Saving the S
The History of the Exmoor Society

Philip Dalling

The Exmoor Society
2020

SAVING THE SPLENDOUR: The History of the Exmoor Society

© Philip Dalling 2020
ISBN 978-1-9997330-4-9

All rights reserved. No part of this publication may be reproduced, stored in a retrieval system, or transmitted, in any form or by any means, electronic, mechanical, photocopying, recording, or otherwise, without the prior permission of the Exmoor Society.

Every effort has been made to trace the copyright holders and obtain permission for quotations and images used. Please do get in touch with any enquiries or any information relating to any images or the rights holder.

*Printed by First Design, Porlock
(www.firstdesignprintweb.co.uk)*

www.exmoorsociety.com

"It is said that the Conservation Movement cut its teeth on Exmoor which, as a relatively soft upland with deeper soils, largely free of rocks, was eminently reclaimable for agriculture. It is exceptional that Exmoor's landscape character and way of life have survived at all and not become like much of the rest of the countryside – homogenised, suburbanised and over-developed. Exmoor remains fragile. It is its National Park status that has protected it and given it international importance."

> Rachel Thomas, CBE, Chairman of the Exmoor Society,
> Presidential Address to The Devonshire Association, 2009

"The first thing to recognise is that there are *multiple* interests in Exmoor – wildlife, amenity, fine scenery, legitimate sports, farming, forestry, and all the other rightful ways of earning a living on the land and in the villages of the moor, including the desire to settle down and retire. The problem is to find a balance between all these interests, so that the result is the best for Exmoor – not sterilising it, not developing it in defiance of what is right. This can be done, if all the interested parties get together and work in liaison, and the Exmoor Society has an important part to play in helping to bring this about."

> Victor Bonham-Carter on assuming
> the Chairmanship of the Exmoor Society in 1966

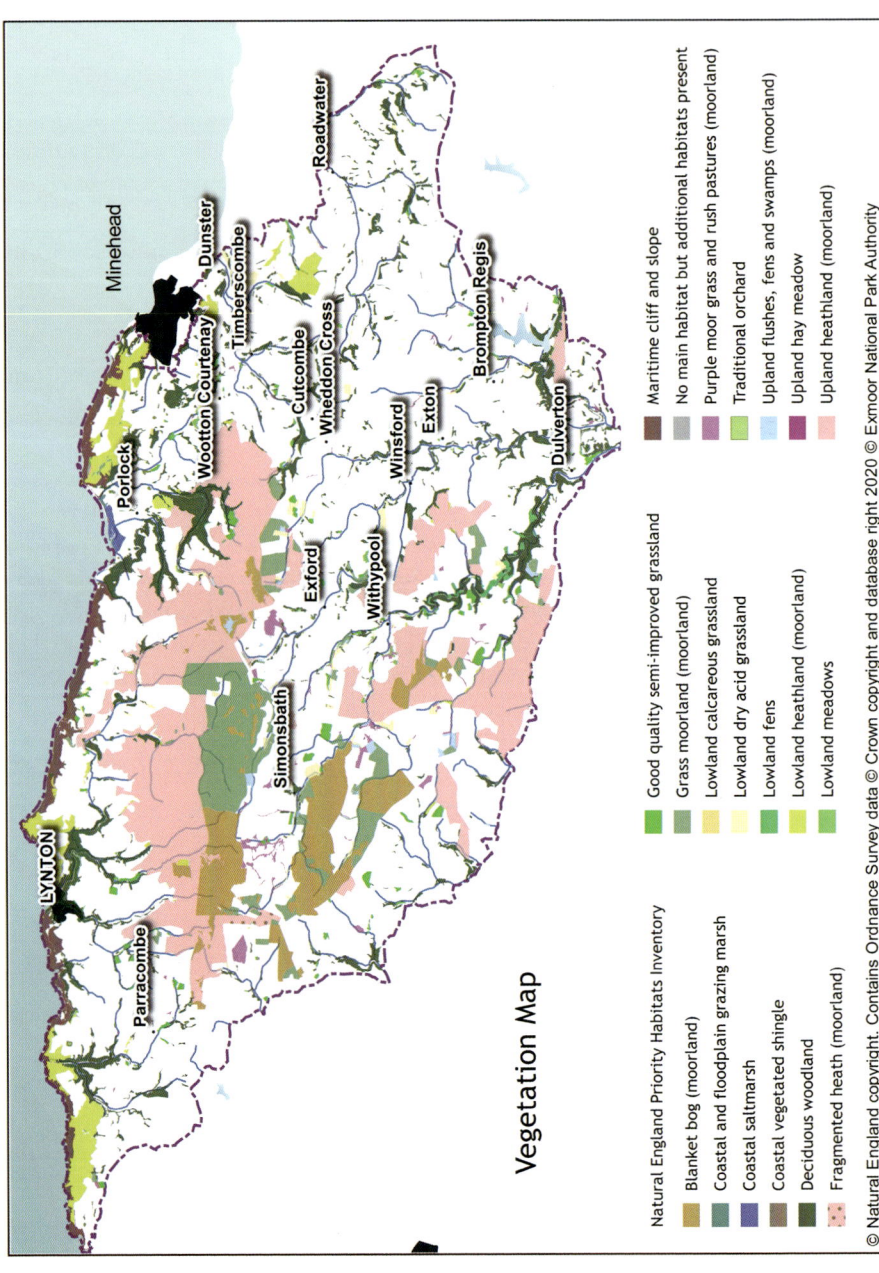

Contents

Foreword by Sir Antony Acland KG — vi
Introduction by Steven Pugsley — vii
Preface and Acknowledgements — ix

PART ONE: GENESIS
Chapter One: Exmoor as a National Park: A Close-run Thing — 1
Chapter Two: The Campaign to save The Chains — 11
Chapter Three: The Exmoor Society is Born — 19

PART TWO: CONFRONTING THE ISSUES
Chapter Four: Defending the Fragile Moorland — 33
Chapter Five: Supporting Upland Farmers — 55
Chapter Six: The Society and Country Sports — 69
Chapter Seven: Welcoming Visitors — 77

PART THREE: THE PRESENT DAY AND INTO THE FUTURE
Chapter Eight: Broadening the Society's Role — 95
Chapter Nine: The Society Today and Tomorrow — 109

Select Bibliography — 124
Note on the Author — 126

Foreword

My earliest known ancestor was a Flemish mercenary called Eccelin who had done useful work for King Henry II and was rewarded with a grant of land near Barnstaple. The name developed from Eccelin to Eccelane, Accelane and finally Acland. An alternative theory is that Henry II expropriated a Saxon called Akka, and Akka's land became Acland.

The family were extremely successful in marrying heiresses who brought them more and more land, the most notable being Elizabeth Dyke who provided land in twenty-two parishes. My wife was born a Dyke but brought no such dowry! And the house in which we now live, Staddon Farm, was part of the growing Acland estates which eventually amounted to 68,000 acres stretching from Barnstaple to Minehead.

So I feel rooted in Exmoor, but my enjoyment comes from other things. Though we have a high rainfall, there are many sparkling days when one can see for miles across the moor. The wildlife is inspiring, with buzzards, curlews and peregrine falcons (the emblem of the Acland family) and of course the wild Exmoor ponies which continue to flourish and might be called the mascot of the moor. The streams and rivers are full of trout, wily though they are to catch. All this makes a wonderful backdrop to country life.

The aim of the Exmoor Society, of which I am proud to be President, is dedicated to preserving the moor. Every planning application is scrutinised to ensure that it does not jar with the moor's natural beauty. But we welcome new initiatives which enable the younger generation to stay and prosper on the moor. It must be a living environment and the Exmoor Society provides funds to encourage useful and beneficial support. The tourism industry is increasingly important. Especially in the spring and summer, Exmoor sees many visitors and it is encouraging that a good proportion enjoy the area and come again from year to year. Long may it all last.

Sir Antony Acland KG,
President of the Exmoor Society

Introduction

For more than sixty years the Exmoor Society has been a significant part of Exmoor life. It is probably true that in its early years it was not always a universally welcome part. Its role of challenge and the strong personalities of some of its leading members meant that relationships with elements of the local population, and indeed the National Park Committee, were occasionally somewhat strained. Arguably, the level of threat to Exmoor's moorlands made a degree of belligerence necessary but it was capable of producing uncomfortable "them and us" positions between the Society and those who regarded themselves as the Exmoor indigenous. As the years have gone by and the concerns of the Society, the National Park Authority and Exmoor land managers have converged, the Society has gained increasing and widespread respect as a body which promotes research to underpin national campaigning, which fosters young entrepreneurship, and which does much to record and protect local history and culture; all of this is in addition to its core task of guarding the Exmoor landscape against desecration of all kinds.

Institutional histories can be numbingly dull. The Society is fortunate that in chronicling its fortunes they have secured Philip Dalling as author. Mr Dalling, being a highly skilled journalist, knows how to cut to the heart of a story and present complex issues in a logical and attractively readable manner. But he knows too that human beings lie at the heart of any organisation, shaping and driving it, and he paints pen-portraits of individuals vividly. The Chairmen in the case of the Exmoor Society are perhaps the most significant and I will, if I may, highlight three from my personal experience.

Victor Bonham-Carter was rigorous, determined, charming, a large presence physically as well as intellectually, whose honesty could be brutal but whose integrity was always beyond doubt. He had chosen to become a farmer for a time on the edge of Exmoor, so he understood the genuine motivation of those who tended the land, but combined that with a sensitivity to landscape and a writing skill that could be lyrical (not for nothing had he been a pupil of Britain's greatest concert pianist, Solomon). All of these he marshalled in defence of Exmoor. Michael Hawkins was an Exmoor man, born and bred in Minehead, but he had been the County Engineer for Devon and consequently brought a business-like precision to the affairs of the Society. As a former local government officer, his great gift was in understanding clearly the parameters within which National Park staff had to work, and knowing when to temper unreasonable expectations on the part of the Society and when to encourage Park employees to go beyond the mundane and realise a grander vision. His term as Chairman marked the turning point in relations between the Park and the Society – the beginnings of rapprochement. Rachel Thomas has guided the Society to its current position of eminence. She has led the physical relocation of the Society to new premises in Dulverton; this has enabled a properly curated archive to be created which, along with the Society's own library, is now a principal resource for the study of Exmoor and its history. With an academic background herself, she has encouraged research which has provided the essential evidence base in making the case at national and regional level for upland landscape and hill farming. The latter is important because under Mrs Thomas's Chairmanship, the Society is encouraging a general understanding that Exmoor is a farmed landscape and that an economically active local population is essential to its survival. That is not to say that the Society embraces every proposal for development, however unsuitable. Far from it. It remains a guardian against the crass and inane, the ugly and the damaging. But it is prepared to be a critical friend and to assist when it should.

There is one further set of individuals who perhaps never quite get the acknowledgement that they should. The Exmoor Society has been singularly blessed in those who have administered its offices and daily business, the unsung heroines (and they have invariably been such) who have ensured that the Society has functioned at the highest degree of efficiency, from figures such as Lindy Harding, through Pauline Bennett, Pat Bawden, to Anne Parham today. With such staff and such leadership, who can doubt that the Exmoor Society will still be flourishing in sixty years' time and the second volume of this history can be written.

Steven Pugsley,
Former Chairman of the
Exmoor National Park Authority

Preface

Walking alone on The Chains, the dominating central plateau of Exmoor, as the morning mist rises to reveal a landscape of austere grandeur, is to experience true isolation and a feeling of communion with the many generations that have shared its solitary splendour.

In the mid-twentieth century there was a proposal to cover The Chains with conifers. Although the concept of National Parks in Britain was already a decade old, conservation was still in its infancy. But the outrage which greeted the plans for The Chains was channelled into a successful campaign to prevent the desecration of an iconic landscape. More than that, it led to the formation of the Exmoor Society. What began effectively as a single-issue protest group quickly broadened its scope and influence to become a positive force for the conservation of all that is good about Exmoor.

Those who walk The Chains today, seven decades later, or simply look up to the plateau from the surrounding valleys, have good reason to be grateful to the Exmoor Society for saving the splendour.

Acknowledgements

Much of my relatively modest knowledge of the Exmoor National Park was gained over the seven-year period in the second decade of the twenty-first century when I was privileged to write a monthly column, entitled 'Man on the Moor', for *Devon Life* magazine. This association opened a great many doors for me within the National Park and so the first expression of thanks must be to the magazine's editor, Andy Cooper, to the deputy editor, Owen Jones, and their colleagues, for making it possible.

One of the doors opened for me was that leading to the Dulverton HQ of the Exmoor Society. It was a rare month indeed when the Society (with its many and varied initiatives and activities) was not a candidate for a share of the space allocated to 'Man on the Moor'. I quickly came to realise what a major and vital role this voluntary body played in the life of the National Park.

Both my personal visits to Dulverton, or frequent hurried telephone calls (when there was a tight deadline), were met with great efficiency and courtesy, both on the part of Society Chairman Rachel Thomas and the members of staff at headquarters, Society Administrator Anne Parham and Assistant Administrator Liz Pile. My thanks for many story leads are due to Dr Helen Blackman, former Outreach Archivist at the Society. I am also grateful to Graeme Bonham-Carter for permission to quote from Victor Bonham-Carter's works, to John Burton and Val Rowlands for permission to quote from S.H. Burton's *Exmoor*, and to Cathy MacEwen for permission to quote from Malcolm MacEwen's writings.

Since being invited to write the history of the Society, I have been privileged to meet many people who have provided information and help. My special thanks go to Mary Chugg, whose memories of the campaign against the afforestation of The Chains and of the early years of the Society have proved invaluable, and to Geoffrey Sinclair for his extremely helpful advice on the chapter on moorland loss and vegetation. I have also had the good fortune to meet trustees, officers and members of the Exmoor Society, too many to name individually. However, my particular thanks go to Rachel Thomas and the members of a working group established to help progress the history project: Society Vice-Chairman Dr Keith Howe, former trustee Caroline Tonson-Rye, and trustees Lisa Eden and Catherine O'Sullivan. Their knowledge, individual professional skills, patience and encouragement have helped to make the task a pleasant one.

Over nearly a decade I have met and been assisted by a great many people at the National Park Authority, both in my capacity as a Standards Committee member and later as a journalist and author. My first article for *Devon Life* was a profile of the then new Chairman of the Authority, Andrea Davis, and I have also enjoyed my contacts with her successor, Robin Milton. Nigel Stone (Chief Executive of the Exmoor National Park Authority during much of the time I have been concerned with the affairs of Exmoor) was unfailingly helpful and I was also able to contribute a profile of his successor, Sarah Bryan, when she first took up her appointment. A special mention must go to Ailsa Stevens, Communications Officer at the National Park Authority, and her predecessor, Clare O'Connor, for their prompt attention to my many queries, and also to Matt Sully for his excellent work on the vegetation map. My thanks also to all the people of Exmoor I have so enjoyed meeting and writing about in the columns of *Devon Life* and in this book.

Finally, sincere thanks to Brenda Dyer. It is well known that writers can become preoccupied and impatient during the birth pains of a new work (some people would just simply say "grumpy") and I owe her a great deal for her patience and forbearance.

Philip Dalling, 2020

PART ONE: Genesis

Chapter One
Exmoor as a National Park: A Close-run Thing

"Tell me what can be the use of a National Park on Exmoor?"
Harold Macmillan, Minister of Housing and Local Government, 1954

Exmoor was designated as a National Park – Britain's seventh – in autumn 1954, pre-dating the Society by four years. The achievement of National Park status was, however, a close-run thing, gained only after much dithering in government circles and in the face of determined opposition from local authorities and landowners.

Any study of the Exmoor Society needs to look in some detail at events in the period between the creation of the National Park and the campaign to save The Chains from afforestation – the catalyst for the formation of the Society. Determined local opposition to National Park status for the moor in 1954 led to compromise in the way the Park was to be administered, and the complicated governance arrangements eventually agreed, deficient in terms of both powers and funding, were to become the cause of bitter disputes over a long period of time.

National Parks' History

When the intention to create a National Park out of the more spectacular areas of West Somerset and North Devon was announced, it immediately sparked a determined campaign to stifle the proposal at birth. Both Somerset and Devon County Councils, fearful of losing control of planning and other issues across a substantial portion of their territories, immediately declared outright opposition.

The Councils were not alone in their opposition. The area of the proposed National Park – which originally included the Quantock range (eventually excluded) – was home to several substantial private estates. The landowners, together with their tenant farmers, were equally opposed to National Park status, believing it would interfere with their ability to manage their own land in their own interests. A majority of the residents of the sparsely populated area that would fall within the boundaries of the proposed Park were, at best, apathetic.

The fierce debate over whether Exmoor should become a National Park culminated in a public inquiry, at the end of which the Government Inspector came out firmly against Exmoor joining the six other areas which had already achieved that status. The final decision would be taken in Whitehall, by Harold Macmillan, then Minister of Housing and Local Government and, on the back of early success as Prime Minister, to be dubbed by cartoonists and political commentators as "SuperMac".

Before looking at the political and bureaucratic intrigues in the corridors of power that surrounded the designation of Exmoor, it is worth examining just exactly what the status of National Park meant (and means) in Britain. The initial concept of the National Park was first proposed in the United States in the 1860s to protect vast, virtually uninhabited wildernesses such as Yellowstone and Yosemite, and the model was later adopted in many other countries.

In Britain the situation was and is very different. Extensive areas of true wilderness are few and far between (except to a degree in Scotland) and most British National Parks include substantial settlements and significant human land use. The land within the boundaries of the Parks remains largely in private hands as opposed to the mainly public ownership found elsewhere in the world. Great Britain has fifteen National Parks – ten in England, three in Wales and two in Scotland – visited annually by 110 million people.

Celebrating wilderness is itself a relatively modern concept. The remote areas of Britain were for long depicted as uncivilised, howling wildernesses by those with the ability and the means to travel, including Daniel Defoe. The author of *Robinson Crusoe* described the Peak District – which in 1951 was the first British National Park to be designated – as "the most desolate, wild and abandoned country in all England". Indeed, it took the writings of the Romantic poets – Shelley, Coleridge and Wordsworth – to popularise the beauty of untamed portions of the national landscape. Their vision nonetheless took more than a century to achieve legal form, with the National Parks and Access to the Countryside Act of 1949. This was celebrated in style in 2019, with Exmoor hosting an event embracing all the British Parks.

After thousands of years of human integration into the landscape, the areas of Britain chosen to receive National Park status differed from their counterparts around the world in the fact that they had been shaped, and were usually maintained and managed by, human activity – typically agriculture, forestry, and field sports. In the 1930s, public interest in the countryside grew, driven in part by a passion for cycle touring and rambling, and by the availability of public transport links between the major conurbations and many attractive areas of the countryside. This enabled the working population to become mobile, but it also generated a growing friction with landowners determined to protect their property and sporting rights.

Several voluntary bodies, some created specifically for the purpose, took up the cause and some embarked upon direct action, notably the 1932 mass trespass on the 2,000-foot-plus high plateau of Kinder Scout in Derbyshire, long dedicated to grouse shooting. This highly politicised protest involved some 400 walkers, who became involved in violent scuffles with gamekeepers employed by the principal landowners. Six protestors were eventually arrested and some received jail sentences.

National Parks' Policy

There was considerable activity throughout the 1930s in the political arena as well as amid the heather and peat bogs of Kinder, and in 1936 a voluntary Standing Committee on National Parks met for the first time. The Second World War meant that the subject was put on ice, but, when peace returned in 1945, John Gordon Dower, an architect, civil servant and secretary of the Standing Committee on National Parks, produced a report that was considered to be the seminal document of the movement.

The Dower Report recommended that a National Park should be an extensive area of beautiful and relatively wild country, existing for the national benefit and meeting four essential criteria, namely that the characteristic natural beauty be strictly preserved, access and facilities for public open air enjoyment be amply provided, wildlife and buildings and places of architectural and historic interest be suitably protected, and established farming use be effectively maintained.

The Attlee Labour government then appointed Sir Arthur Hobhouse to prepare legislation that would eventually make National Parks a reality rather than a dream. Hobhouse recommended that there should be twelve British National Parks and laid down the criteria for choosing their locations:

> The essential requirements ... are that [they] should have great natural beauty, a high value for open-air recreation and substantial continuous extent. [The Parks should be distributed so that] at least one of them is quickly accessible from each of the main centres of population in England and Wales ... there is merit in variety and with the wide diversity of landscape available in England and Wales, it would be wrong to confine the selection of Parks to the more rugged areas of mountain and moorland, and to exclude other districts which, though of less outstanding grandeur and wildness, have their own distinctive beauty and a high recreational value.

SAVING THE SPLENDOUR: *The History of the Exmoor Society*

Mrs M. E. Harper looking out over The Chains, 1958 from a collection held by The Exmoor Society

The grandeur and isolation of the central plateau of Exmoor, The Chains, was one of the prime reasons why the area was deemed worthy in 1954 of the status of National Park. Enthusiastic walkers Richard and Margery Harper loved this wild area and were to play a major role in ensuring its survival in its natural state. Margery is seen looking over the plateau on a wintry day in the 1950s. (Richard Harper, Exmoor Society Archive)

The 1949 Act passed with all party support and the first ten Parks were designated fairly quickly, including Dartmoor in 1951, three years before Exmoor. The land included within the Exmoor Park boundaries was mostly poor-quality agricultural upland. Although much was still owned by individual landowners there was also property owned by public bodies such as the Crown, or charities which allowed and encouraged access, such as the National Trust.

Opposition to the plan for an Exmoor National Park was not solely motivated by the fears of local authorities and the landowners over loss of power and influence. One of the main factors behind the National Park movement was (and is) the desire to make the beauty of natural landscapes available to as many people, of all backgrounds, as possible. Large numbers of visitors bring problems as well as benefits to the areas within National Park boundaries, including erosion of landscape and traffic congestion. They cause conflict over what is the most desirable use of a Park's resources.

Chisel Combe. (By the late Brian Pearce, by kind permission of Elaine Pearce)

Access to cultivated land is restricted to public rights of way and permissive paths, although not all uncultivated areas in England and Wales have the right of access for walking laid down by the most recent relevant legislation, the Countryside and Rights of Way Act of 2000. Today each Park is operated by its own National Park Authority, with two "statutory purposes": to conserve and enhance the natural beauty, wildlife and cultural heritage of the area, and to promote opportunities for the understanding and enjoyment of the Park's special qualities by the public – purposes which at times can perhaps be seen to be contradictory.

National Parks were also eventually given a duty to foster the economic and social wellbeing of the local communities within their boundaries. The varying interpretations of this duty over the years by those who serve on National Park committees, by landowners and farmers, and by public organisations with an interest in conservation, have contributed significantly to often bitter disputes between parties with clashing interests.

The Case of Exmoor
Harold Macmillan needed the wisdom of Solomon rather than the mythic "super powers" ascribed to him by the media to exercise acceptable judgment in the case of the proposal to create the Exmoor Park. It was crystal clear to both the Minister and his Whitehall civil servants that not only was there implacable opposition to the idea locally but, equally, there was little evidence of any groundswell of public opinion clamouring *for* a National Park.

Luccombe is one of Exmoor's most attractive villages, grouped around the parish church of the church of St Mary, which has a chancel dating back to c.1300. (Lisa Eden)

At the public inquiry Devon and Somerset County Councils contended that they were perfectly competent to look after Exmoor. They shrugged off the need for a National Park in the location, saying that Exmoor, unlike Parks such as the Peak District and the Lakes, was not close to major cities and had poor transport links. The authorities called instead for Exmoor to be designated as an Area of Outstanding Natural Beauty (AONB) – a status which would have meant they would have retained all their powers.

The County Councils also claimed that the South West's experience to date of the National Park concept in the form of Dartmoor had not been a happy one. The exact phrase used by the Councils, apt perhaps, given the region's reputation for above-average rainfall, was "the umbrella over Dartmoor National Park had holes in it"! The government-appointed Inspector who conducted the public inquiry obviously agreed with the local authorities; he not only recommended that the Exmoor proposal be rejected, but said that he had not been convinced by the arguments in favour put forward by the Countryside Commission. The Inspector further emphasised his reluctance to support the designation of Exmoor by adding to the typescript of the report the handwritten endorsement "without hesitation".

He also added a curious statement that, "if genders applied, Exmoor would be female, requiring a different approach from Dartmoor, Snowdonia and The Lakes." In the twenty-first century context, it seems a strange and arguably offensive remark. Writing in 1989, after the release of the formerly private paperwork relating to the designation process, Guy Somerset, then Chairman of the Exmoor Society, speculated that the Inspector's comment "was perhaps some hint of the coming rape of the moor by intensive farming".

At the public inquiry virtually the only official local body to favour a National Park was Lynton Urban District Council in North Devon, the nearest thing within the proposed Park boundaries to a traditional "resort". No doubt the Lynton support was given with an eye on the extra visitor numbers the Council believed would result. The final decision now rested with Harold Macmillan, who appeared to be floundering, writing to his senior civil servant asking, "What can be the use of a national park on Exmoor?" The most influential civil servant involved in the debate was Dame Evelyn Sharp (subsequently Baroness Sharp), later to become the first woman to hold the position of Permanent Secretary in a government ministry.

She wrote to Macmillan: "We are all becoming increasingly unhappy about the National Park Commission's steady designation of Park after Park". Her official minute to the minister added that local people on Exmoor were becoming "increasingly bored or worse" about the whole idea. For ministers and officials the National Park movement was "a frightful and unrewarding nuisance"! She added: "It is a great bother but that was the intention of the [National Parks] Act – to make such a bother about unspoilt countryside."

After the inevitable Civil Service practice of going through the possibilities of "on the one hand "and "on the other hand", Dame Evelyn nevertheless advised Macmillan to take account of the political realities of the situation, saying: "Confirmation of the Order [for Exmoor] is the right course. We have to weigh up public opinion. There is no practical importance in confirming the Order but if we refused there really would be a row."

Dame Evelyn, a formidable personality, did not appear to have much sympathy for the National Park concept as a whole. In the urban context, she was a modernist, supporting the demolition of mid-Victorian streets and squares in London and replacing them with high-rise flats. Writing in *The Guardian* newspaper in 2005 the journalist Nick Cohen contended that Dame Evelyn "truly did come close to doing as much damage to Britain as the Luftwaffe in the 1940s".

The National Park lobby, she said, was "small but vocal" and maintained that it could cause ministers a great deal of trouble if they appeared hostile or unsympathetic to the creation of new Parks, adding that not only would it be a "slap in the face" for the National Parks Commission if designation of Exmoor were refused, but it would "create a frightful stir in the press and Parliament".

Macmillan, after weighing the arguments, duly met the National Parks Commission and indicated that he *would* confirm the Exmoor Order against the advice of his Inspector, but on condition that the structure for the new Park's administration was based on three committees, one each for Somerset and Devon (retaining much of the control that the counties had initially feared would be lost), together with a Joint Committee possessing advisory powers only. It is generally held that had this compromise arrangement not been accepted, Macmillan would have backed the view of his Inspector at the public inquiry and rejected National Park status for Exmoor.

Looking back many years later on the manoeuvrings in the months before Exmoor's designation, one of the leading figures in the future Exmoor Society's history was scathing in his criticism of the way in which the National Park administration was structured at its inception. Victor Bonham-Carter – farmer, author and publisher – who was to become Chairman of the Society (his career will be examined in greater detail in Chapter Four), developed his sceptical view through personal experience, as a member of the Somerset Committee and the Joint Advisory Committee for six years from 1956, throughout the period of The Chains controversy and the formation of the Society.

Bonham-Carter initially held back from a close involvement with the Exmoor Society, wishing to avoid a clash of interest. But he quickly realised the shortcomings of the National Park administration and was increasingly drawn towards the Society and its purposes. In *The Essence of Exmoor* (1991) he wrote that "[The National Park administration] made for muddle and procrastination and, apart from routine planning matters, rendered the new Authority powerless to deal with the main issue that bedevilled Exmoor for the next 25 years – land use."

The split committee system as it existed from 1959 to 1968 (and for many years to come) was not an ideal way for the Park administration to gather intelligence about likely threats to the wellbeing of the fledgling National Park, of which the spectre of afforestation of The Chains was a prime example, or of dealing with such a threat in a speedy or efficient manner. Bonham-Carter summed the position up succinctly. Business for the Park Committees, he said, was "slack" in the early days, as pressure upon the

Exmoor has been well served by authors of both fiction (R D Blackmore) and topography. Former Society Chairman and President Victor Bonham-Carter was both author and publisher. Pictured are guests at a party to celebrate the launch of his book The Essence of Exmoor. *Front row, left to right: Clare Court, Mary Pugsley, Steven Pugsley, Victor Bonham-Carter, Ann MacEwen with Malcolm MacEwen behind her, and Paul Hodder-Williams on the right.* (Michael Deering, Exmoor Society Archive)

moorland had not yet become a major problem, and tourism, also to eventually become a significant cause of conflict, was regarded merely as a sideline that brought in some extra cash.

He continued: "Few people at the time expected such a threat to the moor as that posed by the Forestry Commission's proposal for The Chains, and there were immediate and grave doubts as to whether the bodies charged with the protection of Exmoor were fit for purpose when it came to opposing the planned encroachment."

Subsequent battles over land use centred around progressive loss of moorland to the plough, but that was scarcely a live issue at the time the conifer bombshell was dropped. He explained: "At that time no inroads of consequence into the moorland were being made by the hill farmers, who were busy reviving their land and buildings and increasing their stock, assisted by the provisions of the Livestock Rearing Act and other [post-war] Government support."

Bonham-Carter added, however, that there was an important proviso contained within the legislation enabling National Parks that appeared to have given the Forestry Commission hope that afforestation of The Chains came within the bounds of possibility. It was, he said, worth remembering that although the two prime aims of the National Parks Act 1949 were to protect and enhance the landscape of the designated area, and to promote its enjoyment by the public, there was a qualifying clause. That was to the effect that these aims should be pursued "with due regard to the needs of agriculture and *forestry*" [italics added].

For Victor Bonham-Carter, writing in 1991, whatever was responsible for deterring the Forestry Commission from proceeding with its plans for The Chains, it was certainly not the opposition of the Exmoor National Park Committees. He added:

> I am told that The Chains affair was the only "victory" ever won by any National Park against a Government agency for the first twenty years of the [Parks'] existence.

> However, the events of 1958 were not the end of the story, which contained several morals ... that the Exmoor National Park Authority had no teeth, and that the only alternative was to found a voluntary society to act as a watchdog for the future and tell the public what was happening.

Bonham-Carter's criticisms of the Exmoor National Park administration were shared by another man to occupy the position of Chairman of the Society. Guy Somerset, writing in 1986 in the *Exmoor Review*, described the compromise that led to the National Park's initial three-committee structure as "a recipe for bureaucratic delays and inaction". He went on to say:

> Without powers or funds, or a sensible administration, Exmoor was left without any defences. So the loss of moorland continued inexorably for over twenty years. Politicians, civil servants and local authority officials were all opposed to the creation of Exmoor as a national park – and indeed, hostile to or bored with National Parks. It was only the unremitting efforts of the National Park movement that created Exmoor as a Park. The moral is clear for us all today.

Chapter Two
The Campaign to Save the Chains

"Although I was very young at the time, I could see that it was an absolutely barmy idea to plant conifers in that magnificent rolling moorland landscape. We were all new to protest of this kind but we decided to campaign against the Forestry Commission proposal and to recruit other like-minded people to the cause."

Mary Chugg, one of the original campaigners against afforestation of The Chains

In March 1958, just four years after Exmoor was designated a National Park, it emerged that the Forestry Commission, then – as now – a non-ministerial government department responsible for the management of publicly owned forests, was planning to acquire 1,200 acres at The Chains, the moor's central plateau, together with parts of the adjoining Furzehill Common from the owners, the Fortescue Estate. Disfiguring access roads across the moor would be an integral part of the scheme.

The word "emerged" is carefully chosen. The events surrounding the threat to The Chains have today attained almost mythical status and require careful untangling. The legend as it has been passed down across the generations suggests that the plans of the Forestry Commission were leaked by a local planning official to a Barnstaple general practitioner and lover of Exmoor called Dr Richard Harper and his wife Margery.

Today, any such leak would be followed immediately by some active news management on behalf of the Forestry Commission to counter the immense damage caused by the realisation that a public body was secretly proposing a major landscape change in a National Park. But in North Devon in 1958, the effect of the leak, initially, was amazingly low key and few if any public statements by the Commission in its immediate aftermath have come to light.

One justification for the proposal, advanced by the Commission, was that afforestation could help avert a repetition of the disastrous Lynmouth floods of August 1952, which had claimed thirty-four lives. The Chains had been soaked by constant heavy rainfall in the period before the flood and when the water drained from the saturated high ground down the watercourses, it carried disaster in its wake. Nevertheless, some six years after the disaster, the flood-prevention measures put into force were not believed to rely solely on the planting of conifers.

Brian Chugg, Margery Harper and Mary Chugg, 1958. (Exmoor Society Archive)

Brian Chugg leading a school field trip on Exmoor, 1960s. (Mary Chugg)

The Chains Proposal

Richard and Margery Harper's group initially numbered just seven. However, they were remarkably determined and, with little experience of campaigning against powerful national bodies, they decided to take on the might of the Forestry Commission and other vested interests. This led not just to the preservation of a much-loved and ecologically and culturally valuable landscape but, significantly, to the eventual formation of the Exmoor Society, with far-reaching and long-lasting consequences for the wellbeing of the moor.

The Harpers, enthusiastic walkers on Exmoor, were horrified by the proposal and set about mobilising their forces. Two other people with a deep love of Exmoor, Brian and Mary Chugg, both art teachers in Barnstaple, were the first to be recruited. Mary Chugg, twenty-three years old in 1958, is today the sole survivor of the group enlisted by the Harpers, and the only remaining original member of the Exmoor Society. She recalls:

> We had been on holiday abroad when the news broke and Richard and Margery Harper had eagerly awaited our return so we could help oppose the plan. Although we were all new to protest of any kind, we decided we must campaign against the Forestry Commission proposals for The Chains and recruit other like-minded people to the cause.

> It was a cold spring and I vividly remember visiting Maud and Enid Millman, two elderly sisters who shared our horror at the proposals. They lived in an unheated cottage at Cobbaton, on the hills above Swimbridge. We were given a cup of tea but my hands were shaking so much with the cold that it was difficult to drink it. The sisters then recruited a relative at Wootton Courtenay near Minehead, Marjorie Oldham, and so our protest was launched.

> Although I was very young at the time, I could see that it was an absolutely barmy idea to plant conifers in that magnificent rolling moorland landscape. The Forestry Commission's proposals would have created a dark blanket over the landscape and it could not be allowed to happen.

The background to the Forestry Commission's proposal needs some examination. British agriculture, horticulture and forestry changed radically during the twentieth century. The need to feed the population during two periods of total warfare and increase home production of raw materials such as timber, introduced an element of unprecedented governmental influence and control. Nevertheless, there had been no particular indication that the Commission was targeting Exmoor and the plans took the National Park administration of the period and local Councils in the Park's 267 square miles of West Somerset and North Devon by surprise.

It was many years after the events surrounding The Chains saga had become history that a man who ranks as one of the doughtiest campaigners for the integrity of Exmoor, Victor Bonham-Carter, put the 1958 Forestry Commission proposals into their proper context; in his 1991 book, *The Essence of Exmoor*, he described the plan as "an assault from an unexpected quarter".

Leading the Opposition

At this stage the Harpers and their small group kept their response to the proposals low key, mainly confined to identifying figures active locally and nationally in the conservation movement of the time, and to seeking advice on how best to proceed. Equally, the area's local authorities and the National Park administration of the era took some time to recover from the shock caused by the Forestry Commission's plan.

Most feeling was opposed to the afforestation, although at a meeting of Barnstaple Rural District Council (RDC) it was suggested that there was no objection from farmers most closely affected by the scheme, as it was felt the conifers would provide a shelter belt. Another member claimed the farmers in the locality were not opposed to the conifer planting as such, but did fear that the Forestry Commission would demand rights of access across their farms for the construction of the required access roads.

The RDC Chairman, Alderman F.J. Richards, took a sterner line, saying: "We have known Exmoor as a wide open space and thousands go there each year to enjoy the scenery. We must be very careful and jealous of the amenities we possess and see that they are not interfered with in any way."

He added that the area covered by Barnstaple RDC had seen some 500 acres denuded of trees during the 1914-18 war and that land had never been replanted. "The Forestry Commission should plant that derelict land before going on Exmoor", he contended. Local landowner and Rural District Council member Sir Bourchier Wrey of Tawstock Court, near Barnstaple, supported protest against the tree-planting scheme, saying: "It would be a tragedy to plant conifers on Exmoor."

The National Park administration of the time, joined by Somerset and Devon County Councils and rural district councils across West Somerset and North Devon, added its voice to the protests. Just one organisation, the League Against Cruel Sports, actively supported the Forestry Commission proposal, due to its belief that it would seriously hamper hunting on the moor.

The League wrote to the responsible ministries, of Housing and Local Government and Agriculture, asking them to sanction the proposals, saying: "The Exmoor forestry scheme is desirable in every way and the damage, if any, to the National Park amenities will be quite negligible." The League's letter added that most local people wanted the proposals to go ahead because they would provide work for around fifty people for something like three years in an area where there was much winter unemployment.

The debates in council and within the National Park administration at least prompted the two sides in the dispute to take some action. Representatives of the National Park met their counterparts from the Forestry Commission in March up at Brendon Two Gates. Little emerged of any consequence from these talks which, owing to the wintry conditions at a point more than 1,300 feet above sea level and subject to buffeting winds, were not prolonged.

If the way in which the Forestry Commission's proposals had slipped out in the early spring seemed curious, then subsequent developments in the saga were stranger still. Although Dr Harper and his group had been steadily adding supporters and marshalling their arguments, as the summer of 1958 progressed they had still not undertaken any really concrete form of protest (such as a petition), or attempted to enlist the aid of a wider public.

At an official level, discussions were again being held on Exmoor. In early June a meeting took place between the principals involved, with Lord Strang representing the National Parks Commission (the umbrella body for Parks in Britain) and Lord Radnor the Forestry Commission. The landowner, Lord Fortescue, was also present. Then, later in the same month, events occurred which complicated the issue. Not long after this meeting, the deaths were announced of both Fortescues: Lady Fortescue died on 10 June, followed, just four days later, by her husband.

The Forestry Commission put its proposals on ice, although it was made clear that the purchase of The Chains and the planting scheme could still go ahead at some stage. The Harpers and their small band of supporters now had to decide whether, with the immediate threat seemingly at the very least postponed, they should put their campaign on hold and await developments.

Behind the scenes, the group had consulted widely about tactics, and they were advised by several sources nationally and locally to keep up the pressure against the Commission's proposal, despite the scheme being put into abeyance. The consequence was, that on 17 August 1958, their small group, now informally called the "Moor Walkers", stepped up a gear and launched a petition calling for the forestry scheme to be officially withdrawn.

The Lure of The Chains

Any organisation planning a development likely to arouse the ire of lovers of Exmoor could hardly have selected a more controversial site than The Chains. The word iconic may be overused, but when the description is applied to the National Park's majestic central plateau, it is wholly justified.

The Chains is the name given to the north-west plateau of Exmoor, lying above the 1,500 feet (457m) contour line – the highest point is at Chains Barrow (1,597 feet, 487m) and includes the source of the River Barle. It lies roughly within a triangular area of land between Simonsbath, at the heart of the old Exmoor Forest, and the North Devon villages of Challacombe and Lynton.

The Chains is a Geological Conservation Review site, recognised as being nationally important for the landscape transition from ancient, semi-natural woodland through upland heath to blanket mire. The 958 acres of the plateau are owned by the Exmoor National Park Authority and are licensed for grazing. These are the bald statistical details of The Chains. Their description as iconic perhaps owes as much to their powerful impact upon the imagination of the Exmoor lover as to their natural appeal as a majestic landscape feature.

Few who venture into this timeless wilderness can escape an overwhelming feeling of isolation seldom experienced in other lonely places where the distance from human settlement is far greater. The landscape exudes an aura of the distant past for anyone with a heightened awareness of the history, mystery and myth which surround The Chains like the dense hill fogs that often envelop the plateau. Many have come to believe that, far from being empty, this place is still peopled by those who lived and toiled there long ago.

S.H. Burton, whose 1969 acclaimed and scholarly study *Exmoor* won the *Books and Bookmen* Country Book of the Year, recognised the appeal of The Chains to the deeper parts of the human psyche, describing how, when in the vicinity, he felt "an overwhelming sense of antiquity". His sense of time became confused and he realised he was no longer alone. Shadowy figures moved down the track with him, their backs bent beneath great bundles.

A landscape of legend and majestic aspect – though in bad weather often grim – it is one of the few places where a day's walking and exploration of its burial sites and standing stones can be spent without seeing another human being. To the majority of today's observers The Chains in its apparently timeless form is an immutable place.

In Mary Chugg's words:

> I was asked to take the petition [now held in the Exmoor Society's archives] to Barnstaple Pannier Market on a Friday. That was in an era when the stalls were almost all occupied by the wives of farmers and smallholders from across a wide area, including the western parts of the National Park. For the first time in my life I had to stand up publicly for the views I cherished.
>
> Although I spoke mainly to stallholders and gained a lot of signatures, I was often overheard explaining my position by visitors to the area, and they too had many questions to ask. It was not always easy to get the point across. When I was asked what the petition was about, I explained that we were trying to prevent an impressive area of open moorland from being covered with trees and lost forever. Sometimes the response was, "Well, I like trees!" How best to explain that these were the wrong kind of trees!

In addition to circulating the petition as widely as possible, the Harper group staged a public meeting at The Trocadero, a hotel and restaurant in Joy Street, Barnstaple, with a large meeting-room, later replaced by part of the Green Lanes shopping centre. Pictures of The Chains in its unsullied state were shown alongside transparencies produced by Dr Harper and Brian Chugg, depicting some notorious examples of blanket planting of conifers elsewhere, for which the Forestry Commission had been responsible.

As summer turned into autumn, the Moor Walkers group continued collecting signatures for the petition – they eventually totalled some 3,000 – although Richard Harper now went as far as telling the local press that there were some solid indications that the proposal for The Chains might not actually go ahead. The *North Devon Journal Herald* reported on 2 October that there was to be "no let-up on Save Exmoor petition after reports that plan may be withdrawn".

Despite Richard's comments, which the *Journal Herald* does not seem to have pursued with the Forestry Commission, the National Park administration nor the relevant local planning authority, confirmation that the Commission had indeed backed down did not materialise until 27 November, five months after the proposals had actually been put on hold.

Lord Strang of the National Parks Commission was then able to state that the Forestry Commission had withdrawn its plans and had informed the Fortescue Estate of its decision. The reason given by the Commission was the strength of public opinion against the conifer proposal.

Brian Chugg, who in addition to being a talented artist and photographer wrote a highly influential countryside diary for *The Guardian* newspaper, later recalled:

> There were rumours abroad for some time that The Chains was to be saved. We had heard informally that there had been helpful conversations along the "corridors of power". But when the official announcement was made we were still collecting signatures – and had received a few bruises. Nobody failed to attack me, in the press or at my work at North Devon College where I was teaching alongside proponents of economic forestry.

The unaccountable delay in officially lifting the shadow which had hung over Exmoor during those months of 1958 tends to add to the somewhat surreal flavour of the entire episode. The protestors celebrated modestly, with Dr Harper reported by the press as having expressed "relief but not surprise" at the Forestry Commission's decision.

Mary Chugg believes that although the Commission's proposals undeniably caused widespread alarm among lovers of Exmoor, there was always something about the way the organisation handled the plan which did not entirely convince. Was the March 1958 leakage of the proposal simply a means of testing the water to see what sort of public response would ensue? Did the Commission realise at some stage that the proposals were not economically viable?

Nevertheless, the realisation that Exmoor was likely to face further and perhaps more serious threats led the Harper group and other Exmoor enthusiasts to begin to consider the desirability of forming a permanent organisation to help protect the moor. The active protestors and sympathisers who had been awakened to the potential threats by The Chains issue had, at that time (and well into the future), little confidence in the National Park administration's ability to adequately defend its territory.

Walkers on the moor, 1950s, believed to be Margery Harper (with the dog) and her two children.
(Richard Harper, Exmoor Society Archive)

Chapter Three
The Exmoor Society is Born

"We were all aware after The Chains affair that we had won a battle, but not the war. It was apparent that the conifer plan would not be the last threat to the Exmoor landscape and something more than a one-off campaign like our petition, however successful it had proved, would not be sufficient in the future. We had to keep going and lay the foundations for an organisation that would be capable of fighting Exmoor's corner, no matter from which direction the threat emerged."

Mary Chugg

The wealth of published material which issued from the Exmoor Society from its birth in the autumn of 1958 and continued throughout the early years of its existence is remarkable for the amount of military metaphor that it contains.

The Society was born out of "the *fight* for The Chains" and was soon plunged into a decades-long *struggle* to save its surviving moorland from the plough. But these two campaigns were simply the stand-out headline events of the 1960s, '70s and '80s. For during that long and testing period even routine Society documents and the columns of its journal, the *Exmoor Review*, were littered with words with a warlike flavour, such as *battle*, *conflict* and *tension*.

With the benefit of hindsight, it is not really surprising that such should be the case. On both sides of the arguments that raged over Exmoor were men (and some women) whose talents and abilities – and a sense of determination to press affairs to a conclusion – had been honed in the major twentieth-century wars of 1914-18 and 1939-45, not to mention the smaller colonial struggles of the time.

When the contest over The Chains took place the protagonists with war experience, particularly but not exclusively in the Second World War, provided a majority of the leading players – men (usually) who were serious individuals, still vigorous and in the prime of life, all imbued with a determination to do their duty according to their own lights. The rank-and-file membership lists of the Society too were well padded with former officers from the Armed Forces, who had retired to West Somerset and North Devon but were more than ready to flock back to the colours when they feared the whole concept of the National Park they loved was in peril.

So where can an analogy be drawn with the landowners and tenant farmers who backed reclamation of moorland, afforestation and other schemes that were anathema to the Society? Surely this group for the most part lacked a recent military background? Their contribution (albeit a vital one) to the war effort had been fought on the home front, helping to ensure that a nation with its back to the wall was adequately fed.

It is easily forgotten that these same landowners and farmers had developed substantial campaigning skills of their own in dealing with the extra layers of bureaucratic control and tight legislation that had proved necessary during wartime. They could and would prove to be formidable opponents even when faced with the experienced and dedicated conservationists who would come to form the Society's "big guns", in the form of S.H. "Tim" Burton, Victor Bonham-Carter, John Coleman-Cooke and, at a later date, Malcolm MacEwen.

A considerable element behind the conflict between the Society and the landowners and farmers had been the not unreasonable desire of the latter group to shake off many of the more irksome controls imposed in wartime. By the late 1950s, for most of the population the worst aspects of wartime controls, usually imposed with a shrug and the reminder, "well, there is a war on", had disappeared, together with much of the additional bureaucracy of the war years and of the post-war austerity which followed victory.

Landowners and tenants who had long been subject to the enhanced 1940s strictures of the Ministry of Agriculture and the War Agriculture Committees had been expecting a gradual relaxation of controls and a return to something like a situation where, in their plaintive and oft-repeated phrase, a farmer, within reason, could "do what he liked with his own land".

Hill farmers in particular, with justification, wanted to share in the increasing prosperity exemplified in the pronouncement by Harold Macmillan, who became Prime Minister in January 1957, that "most of our people have never had it so good". Macmillan was a landowner himself with a 1,200-acre estate, Birch Grove, in Sussex.

The landowning class, and the tenant farmers – the latter often struggling to make a living in the harsh conditions of Exmoor – could perhaps be forgiven for not responding kindly to being told what they could and could not do by conservationists (still a rare species in the 1950s). The case for the landowners and the tenant farmers was strengthened by the clause in the 1949 Act that established Britain's National Parks, which emphasised that decisions taken by Park authorities must pay heed to the needs of agriculture and forestry.

Chapter Three: The Exmoor Society is Born

During the months between the announcement that the conservationists' view had prevailed over the Forestry Commission's initial intention to plant conifers on The Chains, the initiative for the formation of a Society was taken by naturalist, conservationist and author John Coleman-Cooke. He had provided wise counsel to the group led by Dr Richard Harper during the campaign to preserve The Chains.

Sensing that the threat was to the moorland as a whole, not simply to individual sections, he called a meeting at his home, Simonsbath Lodge, in the heart of the old Exmoor Forest, on 29 October 1958. Coleman-Cooke convened the steering committee that led to the formation of the Exmoor Society, and was soon elected as the group's first Chairman. He had discovered the house, which he rented from the Fortescue family, soon after the end of the Second World War, in which he served as a major in the British Army.

John Coleman-Cooke, the founder of the Exmoor Society. (Exmoor Society Archive)

Simonsbath Lodge, built in 1654, the venue for the first meeting of the Exmoor Society. (ENPA)

The discovery had been made in a fashion particularly apt for Exmoor, whilst he was riding across the moor from village to village on what a groom at Dulverton had described as a "gassy puller", later recalling that this was "a brutally therapeutic exercise after nine years out of the saddle". Coleman-Cooke went on to explain:

> If immediately you feel at home in an empty house, then the logical course is to occupy it. The proposition left my wife speechless; but I argued that it was the quality and not the quantity of rooms that mattered. Living there was soon seen to be in the nature of a traditional preferment. You automatically occupied a niche, and if sometimes you felt rather like an outdated statue, the long panelled rooms were ideal for writing and meditating in.

The new Society quickly became a branch of the Council for the Preservation of Rural England (CPRE) – an organisation formed in 1926, and re-named in the 1960s as the Council for the Protection of Rural England. The Society became a charity in its own right in the 1980s.

Movers and Shakers

The early linkage with the CPRE, one of the longest-running environmental groups in existence, was an astute move on the part of the founders of the Exmoor Society. It gave the fledgling Society an immediate national standing, encouraged Sir Gonne Pilcher, a distinguished High Court judge, to become its first President, and attracted many more vigorous and enthusiastic personalities into membership, with the first wave of recruits including John Goodland, who became the first editor of the *Review* and succeeded Coleman-Cooke as Chairman in 1964.

Sir Gonne St Clair Pilcher was in a good position to represent the new Society in the higher reaches of the British establishment. After his retirement from the bench he came to live in Lynch, Allerford, in Somerset, and his entry in *Who's Who?* showed his main recreational interest as being the archetypal Exmoor pastime of hunting. Born in 1890, he was called to the Bar in 1915 and became King's Counsel in 1936. For a spell in 1938 he was deputy chairman of Somerset Quarter Sessions. He was knighted in 1942. In common with so many of the people with whom he would have dealt both within the Society and elsewhere, he had enjoyed a distinguished service career. He served in France and Belgium between 1914 and 1918, was mentioned in despatches and was awarded the Military Cross.

As the Society steadily gained in membership and in campaigning experience, personalities emerged who would play a major role in the turbulent years ahead although, as mentioned earlier, there was at first a tendency among some individuals to hold back from activism within the Society fearing a clash of interests.

Victor Bonham-Carter and Tim Burton were both members of Exmoor National Park committees and initially felt that their positions precluded them from too deep an involvement with the Society. Similarly, Derick Heathcoat-Amory, Member of Parliament for Tiverton from 1945 to 1960 and Chancellor of the Exchequer in Macmillan's government, declined to be considered for the office of Society President. Bonham-Carter and Burton maintained this semi-detached stance until the frustrations of membership of the National Park committees forced them to take a more active role in the campaigning over land reclamation.

The people who helped shape the Exmoor Society and drive forward its campaigns had from the start a most effective platform for propagating their views. One of the Society's first concrete actions was to launch the *Exmoor Review*, which still thrives in 2020. The personalities of the Society's first stalwarts shine from the pages of this journal, which from the start has been not just a record of an organisation's activities but a countryside magazine ranking with the best in the field. John Goodland edited the first four editions of the *Review* (the very first of which appears here, right), before exchanging jobs with John Coleman-Cooke.

Coleman-Cooke himself was active in helping the National Trust acquire Heddon's Mouth in 1965 and Woody Bay in 1966, with the Exmoor Society, now rapidly growing in numbers and influence, able to contribute £5,000 and £1,000 to the respective purchases. In subsequent years John Coleman-Cooke concentrated on his career as a freelance writer. He wrote many articles, critiques and reviews for the *Western Morning News*, *The Field*, the *North Devon Journal Herald* and other periodicals, mainly on wildlife and the countryside. His books included *Discovery II in the Antarctic* and *The Harvest that Kills*.

He also contributed several articles to the *Review* of great interest and of considerable relevance to the early campaigns fought by the Society in the field of conservation. One outstanding example, in 1963, was entitled 'Black Grouse on Exmoor' and described the decline of the game bird – a decline principally traceable to the destruction of its moorland habitat by arable farming.

Another major contribution Coleman-Cooke made during this period emphasised that the Society and its founders were as much concerned with preserving the cultural life of the National Park as with conserving its natural fabric. He published a vivid and first-hand account of local life soon after the end of the Second World War, describing how, with no television, no regular bus service, and with only a few families owning cars, people foregathered for communal entertainment. Amateur theatricals were particularly popular, but given the closeness of the rural communities and the fact that most people not only knew each other very well but were often related, the plays had to be carefully chosen:

> Too much emphasis on death, or on a plot that laid unhealthy stress on a son or daughter in serious trouble, or a husband or wife misbehaving with somebody else's partner – such happenings (when dramatised) could – and sometimes did – shake the very foundations of the community, and present insuperable problems in casting. The love scenes were especially tricky. If you didn't throw yourself into them with zest they seemed wooden, and if you did the rumours began ...

Towards the end of his life, Coleman-Cooke lived in lodgings in London's Notting Hill Gate, completing a politico-military study, *Uncivil Wars*, for the publisher Michael Joseph. He found this task very hard going, and the difficulty of it induced a long period of depression and may have contributed to his death from heart failure in 1978 at the age of sixty-four. The manuscript was never published.

Present at the inaugural meeting of the Society and providing support for Coleman-Cooke during the early years were the members of the ad-hoc group which had come together to fight for The Chains. Mary Chugg recalls:

> We were all aware after The Chains affair that we had won a battle, but not the war. It was apparent that the conifer plan would not be the last threat to the Exmoor landscape and something more than a one-off campaign like our petition, however successful it had proved, would not be sufficient in the future. We had to keep going and lay the foundations for an organisation that would be capable of fighting Exmoor's corner, no matter from which direction the threat emerged.

The story of the moorland campaigns of the 1960s and 1970s will be related in detail in Chapter Four. But despite the immense pressure on its officers to keep the momentum alive and hold off numerous threats to the landscape of the moor, other issues were not neglected.

The names on the first membership list are revealing. The vast majority were drawn from the South West, but there was a fair representation from

London, as well as from Kent, Sussex, Norfolk, Cardiff – with several names (probably from the same family) from The Mumbles, near Swansea – a number from Burton-on-Trent, and one from Nottingham, the furthest point north recorded.

In later years the list of vice-presidents (none were recorded in 1959) was to feature several local Members of Parliament although in the first published list, Edward Du Cann, MP for Taunton, and later a minister and a long-serving Chairman of the Conservative Party, was simply a "guinea member". Society membership at that time had a two-tier structure. Payment of a subscription of one guinea granted membership of both the CPRE and the Exmoor Society. A subscription of five shillings a year brought membership of the Society alone. Both grades of membership entitled the subscriber to a copy of the *Exmoor Review*. Military ranks, as mentioned previously, appeared frequently and there was one foreign-based member, from Demerara in British Guinea.

Bonham-Carter and Burton were not absent from the ranks of Society activists for very long; any scruples they possessed about the propriety of having one foot in the "official" ranks of the National Park administration whilst at the same time helping to lead opposition to Park policies with which they strongly disagreed soon went out of the window.

They were to make a formidable triumvirate when joined by Malcolm MacEwen, a conservationist of national and international repute. Bonham-Carter and Burton had long connections with Exmoor and its specific issues; MacEwen had fought his earlier battles on a national front. In retirement at Wootton Courtenay on Exmoor, he became gradually more and more involved in the affairs of the Society. Eventually he took a ministerial appointment to the Exmoor Park's governing body, where he occupied a generally solitary role, attracting considerable personal abuse on account of his unrelenting commitment to the cause of conservation and for his political standpoint.

The campaigns and the writings of Bonham-Carter, Burton and MacEwen, and the crucial roles they played in the battles for the survival of what had made Exmoor special and worthy of designation as a National Park, will be examined in depth in succeeding chapters. However, it is worthwhile at this point to look at the characters and careers of the three as individuals. Each adhered to a political standpoint to the left of centre – very considerably to the left of the majority of Exmoor landowners and of most of those on the three committees that made up the National Park administration of the day.

The commitment of the three main Society activists to the cause of conservation and their stubborn refusal to bow the knee to authority when convinced it was misguided or venal in its approach, ensured that there would be no surrender to those who saw Exmoor simply as a development opportunity. Nevertheless it is clear from their writings that Burton and MacEwen were often pessimistic, even despairing, about the future of the National Park. Bonham-Carter's view was tempered by an understanding of the needs of those who lived and worked on the moor. In the final analysis, their persistence and guiding principles ensured that the Exmoor Society could never become simply a type of supporters' club, a group of cheerleaders for the National Park administration, in whatever format it existed.

In 2020, when the relationship between the Society and the modern Exmoor National Park Authority (ENPA) is wholly cordial, and the two bodies, together with newer organisations like the Exmoor Hill Farming Network, co-operate extensively in various initiatives designed for the wellbeing and advancement of the Park, the Society's role remains what it has been for six decades: a critical friend, with the emphasis on the word "friend".

Given the circumstances at the point of formation, and the battles to come, it was perhaps just as well that the Society's leading figures were old campaigners in every sense of the word. Samuel Holroyd Burton, always known as "Tim", Chairman of the Society from 1966 to 1971, was typical of the generation born just after the First World War whose socialism and anti-fascism led them to volunteer for the Army in 1939. He was invalided out of the service in 1941, having been nursed in a military hospital by his future wife, Phyl.

Burton combined being head of the English department at Blundell's School, Tiverton, with a distinguished career as an author of books on topography, biography, criticism,

S.H. "Tim" Burton, a former Chairman of the Exmoor Society, pictured in 1964 at Blundell's School, Tiverton, where he was head of the English Department. (Tiverton Gazette)

fiction, as well as anthologies and editions of the Classics and English as a foreign language textbooks. Many people might best be aware of Tim Burton through his authorship of one of the definitive works on the National Park and its surroundings, entitled simply *Exmoor* and first published in 1952, eventually running into several editions. He was a staunch campaigner, not just for Exmoor, but for a variety of causes, and his published comments about those with whom he clashed could be caustic.

He was a leading figure in the establishment of a branch of the Campaign for Nuclear Disarmament (CND) in Tiverton, a town perhaps not renowned for its radicalism. He remained a supporter of the Labour Party until his death in 2005 at the age of eighty-six. His son, John Burton, who contributed an obituary to *The Guardian* newspaper, put the situation into context; his father, he emphasised, was a supporter of "Old Labour" and not an admirer of the "New" Blairite Labour party.

Victor Bonham-Carter had links to the Bonham-Carter political dynasty, notable for its politicians and military men. An internet entry for the family lists some thirty members including Laura Bonham-Carter, the daughter of Liberal politician Violet Asquith and the granddaughter of Liberal Prime Minister H.H. Asquith. Laura was an elder sister of Mark Bonham-Carter, the winner of one of the Liberal Party's best-known by-election victories, at Torrington, North Devon, in 1958. Her niece is the actress Helena Bonham-Carter. Laura continued the family's Liberal tradition by marrying Jo Grimond (later Lord Grimond), leader of the Liberals from 1956 to 1967. Grimond's successor as Liberal leader was Jeremy Thorpe, whom the Bonham-Carters had introduced to the North Devon constituency in 1952. As a Vice-President of the Society Thorpe was rather more than a figurehead, proving to be a regular visitor and occasional speaker at Society gatherings.

Despite the political pedigree of the name he bore, Victor Bonham-Carter had little interest in national politics, although the many books that he wrote included *In a Liberal Tradition*, a history of the Bonham-Carter family, written using documents dating back to the seventeenth century. But on local issues, both within his parish council (at East Anstey) and, across the broader acres of Exmoor, it was a different matter altogether. Victor enjoyed a varied career as an author, farmer and publisher. His principal interests lay in the countryside and military history, but he also spent a significant part of his life helping his fellow writers, through the Society of Authors, which represented the interests of some 8,000 professional writers. He played a leading role in the Society's campaign in the 1970s to secure public lending rights.

In the 1950s he ran a mixed farm in Somerset, on the fringe of the National Park, was the historian of the Dartington Hall estate, in Devon, established in the 1930s as a social experiment in resuscitating a rural community, and wrote a number of books about rural matters, including *The English Village* and *Farming the Land*, a textbook for secondary school children, *The Survival of the English Countryside*, an analysis of the historical changes in land use which addressed what would now be described as environmental issues, and *The Essence of Exmoor*.

In 1969 Bonham-Carter started a publishing company at Dulverton called Exmoor Press, to publish the *Exmoor Review* and a series of 50-page micro studies, each written by an expert, about life on the moor and some of which remain in print. He died in March 2007, aged ninety-three, prompting current Exmoor Society Chairman Rachel Thomas to tell the congregation at his memorial service that:

> Nobody should underestimate the richness of the legacy that Victor Bonham-Carter has left to the Exmoor Society and to Exmoor. He was a man for all seasons, staying with the Society through exciting and ordinary times, through difficult and sometimes acrimonious times, through wet winters and warm springs, for over 60 years from his first arrival on Exmoor, to a small hill farm, just outside Dulverton, in 1947.
>
> Victor used his rare combination of talents as a campaigner, writer, broadcaster, teacher, farmer and publisher to promote the Society and its cause of protecting Exmoor as a National Park. Victor was a visionary who saw clearly the important role of voluntary bodies like the Exmoor Society. He recognised that they had no statutory clout but depended on powers of persuasion, efficiency in lobbying and ability to brief and convince the public. Public opinion, he said, sooner or later influenced those in power. His concerns over Exmoor's loss of moorland, essential to its National Park status, led to him becoming actively involved at different times in all the main offices of the Society: a member of the executive, then chairman, followed by president, and sometime editor of the *Exmoor Review*.

Much further to the left in terms of his personal politics than the socialist Tim Burton was Malcolm MacEwen, whose reputation as a leader in the relatively new field of conservation was truly international. Like Bonham-Carter and Burton, MacEwen had, at times, a foot in both Exmoor camps. For eight years from November 1973 he was a ministerial appointment to the re-organised National Park administration – appointed, ironically and somewhat to his surprise, by a Conservative government. During this period he was a member of the Society's executive committee and, for five years (1974-78), was joint editor of the *Review* with Hilary Binding. He later became Vice-President of the Society, sharing the honour with an Anglican Bishop and two Tory MPs.

Malcolm MacEwen's obituary in 1996, which like Burton's appeared in *The Independent*, described him as "a revolutionary twice over, first as a Communist and second as a trenchant critic of our wasteful, high-energy and polluted way of life." He was born into a political household – his father was a pioneer of the Scottish Nationalist Party – but whilst at Edinburgh University Malcolm became a card-carrying member of the CP. His first party role was as office lawyer on the Glasgow version of the *Daily Worker*. Then he moved to the post of party secretary in north-east England before returning to the *Worker*, this time in London. His own experience of warfare came as a foreign correspondent for the *Daily Worker*, when he witnessed the post-Second World War conflict between Greek Left and Royalist forces backed by the British Army (and, it needs to be said, by the Labour government headed by Clement Attlee).

Like many others, MacEwen left the Communist Party around the time of the Hungarian uprising in 1956 and worked for first *The Architectural Review* – once the journalistic home of another noted conservationist in the shape of John Betjeman – and later for the Royal Institute of British Architects, eventually becoming the organisation's Director of Public Affairs. His connection with Exmoor began when he retired to Somerset and received the appointment to the Exmoor National Park's governing body.

Whether the appointing minister at the time realised what a bombshell he was planting in the Authority's very midst is unclear. *The Independent*'s obituarist summed it up in the following way: "[MacEwen's] fellow members were actively conniving in the ploughing-out of that very moorland the Park was supposed to conserve. MacEwen successfully made a public scandal of this, survived several years of vilification by the landowners and renters [tenant farmers] and was vindicated by an ensuing official inquiry."

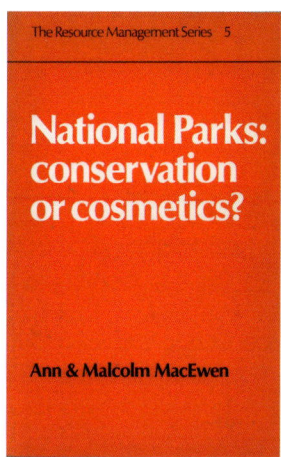

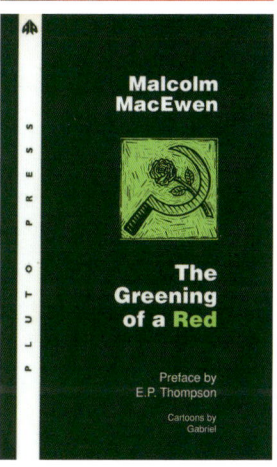

Top: National Parks: Conservation or Cosmetics?, *1982. The Guardian's obituary of Ann MacEwen said that this book "gave the national parks movement an intellectual basis it had lacked".*
Above: *MacEwen's autobiography,* The Greening of a Red, *appeared in 1991.*
(Both Exmoor Society)

Chapter Three: The Exmoor Society is Born

Launching the Exmoor Museum

Perhaps the Society's most notable success in the early years was the creation and initial management of the Lyn and Exmoor Museum in Lynton. The idea of a museum came from Society members, inspired by the successful staging of a series of village exhibitions in Bratton Fleming, Winsford, Porlock and elsewhere, with exhibits ranging from Stone Age implements to the work of modern craftsmen.

Society members in Lynton quickly realised that a suitable home for such a museum was available. St Vincent's House, close to Lynton's Market Hall, was one of the town's oldest buildings, and of considerable social and architectural interest in its own right, possessing a rare stone slab roof. The building had been condemned as unfit for continuing human habitation and was threatened with demolition. Its owner, Lynton Urban District Council, was nevertheless well aware of its interest and handed over control of the building, at a peppercorn rent, to the Exmoor Society, which had resolved to sponsor the museum project.

John Goodland put his finger on the importance of such an undertaking to the Society. In the 1961 issue of the *Review*, he wrote: "A great burden of work will fall on us, but also great credit if the work is done well. This will

The Lyn and Exmoor Museum, an early Society initiative. (Exmoor Society Archive)

View of Lynton (ENPA).

be something tangible and will help our transition from being a small band of idealists to being a body with responsibilities and cares."

The sub-committee charged with driving the museum project was chaired by John Pedder, a Society trustee. A member of Lynton Urban District Council and later Chairman of North Devon District Council, he came from a long-established local business family, succeeding his father as postmaster and a great advocate of the attractions of the twin-towns.

Pedder and fellow enthusiasts restored and redecorated the property to prepare the museum for its opening, often toiling until midnight. The object was to introduce the National Park to visitors and provide an outlet for the zeal of local archaeologists, antiquarians and naturalists, portraying a picture of the life, trade, crafts, and customs of Exmoor in the past. A main feature was a replica of a typical eighteenth-century Exmoor kitchen, with open fireplace, wainscoting, a settle, and old beams, reconstructed as a gift by Mr Bob Nancekivell. Village stocks were installed in the garden and a collection of ancient farm implements and craft tools were on display.

Initial requests for funding were rejected by many bodies, although there were grants from the Devon Exmoor National Park Committee and the Society itself. Undaunted, the museum enthusiasts set about raising their own funds, and among the private donors – not for the first time in the case of an Exmoor cause – was holiday camp tycoon Billy Butlin. The original admission fee was six old pence and within two years of operation the visitors' book held some 2,000 signatures, including those of parties of overseas students organised by the British Council.

The obituarist added that it was natural for MacEwen and his second wife, Ann, to thereafter become joint gurus of the National Park movement, saying: "The couple's first book on the subject *National Parks: Conservation or Cosmetics?* (1982) is still the best in the field. It is outstanding for marrying sympathy for landscapes with an understanding of the needs of the people who make their livings in the parks and the awkwardnesses of the administrative structures by which the parks are run."

No apology needs to be made for singling out Bonham-Carter, Burton and MacEwen as the outstanding personalities of the earlier decades of the Exmoor Society. They lived in what the well-known Chinese proverb would call interesting times and never shirked controversy. Together with the group that gathered around Dr Richard Harper, with John Coleman-Cooke and Guy Somerset (to date still the Society's longest-serving Chairman), they are assured of an honoured place in the organisation's history.

A great many more people – too many to name – made vital contributions to the successes the Society enjoyed – successes that ensured Exmoor's continuing credibility as a National Park. All through the times of struggle and amid the very real threats to the fabric of the moor, the Society nevertheless managed to pay due attention to a wide variety of other issues. The management of an increasing number of visitors, the threatened encroachment of suburbanisation in some areas of the National Park, and the need to encourage suitable light industry to provide much-needed employment and prevent young people from being forced to move away from the moor, were high on the list of priorities.

Through the medium of competitions and awards, and through the columns of the *Review*, the Society encouraged cultural and social activities. To match its growing stature, it also acquired a headquarters, in the form of the Parish Rooms in Dulverton, which provided a venue for meetings and a location for its at first small but steadily increasing archive of material relating to Exmoor. The Society's growing membership over the years led to the formation of a London branch and local groups in other centres, including Bristol, Barnstaple, South Molton, Porlock and Dulverton.

With the Society firmly established as the tumultuous decade of the 1960s dawned, it is time to move the focus of its history on to a detailed examination of the issues that dominated officers and members for more than twenty years – the critical battles to preserve the landscape of Exmoor. Had the Society not achieved great success in its campaigns against the loss of precious moorland, the National Park would have been severely damaged, putting in doubt its survival into the twenty-first century, at least in any meaningful form. Had the National Park been reduced to a state hardly worthy of the title, the status of the Society too would surely have been diminished.

PART TWO: Confronting the Issues

Chapter Four
Defending the Fragile Moorland

"During this time several thousand acres of heather and grass moorland were lost to the plough ... [areas] valuable for their flora, birds and mammals, and enjoyed by walkers and riders."

Victor Bonham-Carter, *The Essence of Exmoor*

To gain anything like a full understanding of the often bitter conflicts which arose between the Exmoor Society and the Exmoor National Park administration over the issue of land use and moorland reclamation during the early years of the Society's existence, it is necessary to study in detail the complex and unwieldy structure devised for the governance of the Park on its creation in 1954.

The account contained in Chapter One of how Exmoor's claim to National Park status was very nearly denied by the government emphasised the opposition to that status mounted by both Somerset and Devon County Councils, who objected to the loss of powers they feared it would bring. The two County Councils were joined in their opposition by the rural district councils covering West Somerset and North Devon and, tellingly, by the vast majority of landowners whose estates and farms lay within the Park's boundaries, and who feared interference with their ability to use that land in any way they thought fit.

When the government of the day *did* eventually consent to Exmoor becoming a National Park, the responsibility for its policy making and day-to-day administration was effectively left in the hands of the two County Councils, the very bodies which had led the opposition to the Park's creation. Initially a tripartite structure was imposed, with three committees. The actual decisions (including planning matters) were to be made by separate county committees, for Somerset (which contained roughly two-thirds of the Park's acreage) and for Devon (which accounted for the remaining third). The structure allowed for an additional joint committee, which had advisory powers only.

Change was a long time coming. When local government was reorganised in the early 1970s the structure was amended, but in reality little really altered and local government retained control. Instead of two county committees and an advisory committee, the revised Exmoor National Park governing body became a committee of Somerset County Council, with representation from Devon. Two-thirds of the members of the committee were elected councillors from each side of the county boundary, with the remaining third consisting of people appointed by the responsible government minister (by that time the Secretary of State for the Environment) to look after what was described as "the national interest". This group included the Society's Malcolm MacEwen.

It was at this point that the National Park acquired a base within its boundaries, at Exmoor House, Dulverton (Park headquarters to this day) and a National Park Officer was appointed to head up the organisation and manage a small team of staff. The reorganisation, and particularly the establishment of a headquarters within the Park, was seen by the Exmoor Society's strategists as representing a qualified step forward, but the powers (and, crucially, the funding) long demanded for the authority by the Society were still not in place.

It was not until nearly a quarter of a century had elapsed before the Park's administration won its independence from local government in the 1995 Environment Act. In April 1997, in a move genuinely welcomed by the Exmoor Society, the present-day Exmoor National Park Authority (ENPA) was established as an independent public authority, with responsibility for managing its own budget and a full range of activities, including a vital planning role. The major contribution to that budget comes from the central government Department for Environment, Food and Rural Affairs (Defra).

Returning to the 1960s, the original National Park governing structure was considered by the Society to have very limited powers and resources, legally and financially. The administration was seriously constrained too by the insertion of a clause in the legislation which established National Parks (the 1949 Act) stipulating that all decisions needed to take *"due regard to the needs of agriculture and forestry"* within the Park boundaries.

This clause, giving what the conservation lobby saw as an undue weighting in favour of the landed interest, and the preponderance of landowners (including farmers who owned their own land) on the Exmoor Park committees, created favourable conditions for those who wished to reclaim, by ploughing or other "improvements", much of the characteristic moorland which still survived.

The relatively new Society found itself up against both the official powers of the Park administration (driven by the two County Councils) and the attitudes of the vast majority of the body's members – which varied from, at best, suspicion of what many regarded as a group of meddling outsiders to, at worst, downright hostility.

During these difficult years the Society needed activists with equal measures of determination and persistence to continue to promote their beliefs in the face of that suspicion and hostility. At the heart of the Society's campaigning was the previously mentioned hardcore of determined individuals: Victor Bonham-Carter, Tim Burton and Malcolm MacEwen. MacEwen's wife Ann was also a dedicated conservationist and the group was joined by others, notably Guy Somerset, who was to chair the Society for twenty years in the period of bitterest conflict.

These leading figures, their Society colleagues and many distinguished and talented people from outside the moor, who brought their individual knowledge and expertise to the struggle, shared a common belief that the spirit of the 1949 Act, if not the actual letter, should favour preservation of the natural features of the moor and better access for the public above commercial interests.

Each individual Society activist brought something of value to the table. Bonham-Carter had for a while in the years following the Second World War been a farmer. While he never wavered in his commitment to conservation, his experience of agriculture in and around Exmoor gave him a practical understanding of the difficulties faced by those whose livelihood was derived from the land and, perhaps, a certain degree of credibility among the landowning and farming communities that some other leading Society figures lacked.

Malcolm MacEwen's great virtue was his steadfastness as a campaigner, coupled with his political acuity. Becoming aware in the early 1970s of the forthcoming reorganisation of Park administrations, with the accompanying innovation of Secretary of State appointees drawn from outside the old magic circle of local councillors and landowners, he set about establishing himself as a widely recognised figure within the Parks movement. He realised that, if successful in securing an appointment, his views would continue to place him in a minority in the Exmoor meeting-rooms and he reasoned that he would struggle to achieve anything worthwhile unless he could become "the best informed member of the Authority", and could forge strong links with the national conservation movement and the local and national media.

MacEwen established his *bona fides* through his work in radio and newspaper journalism, and by his close involvement with a campaign mounted to expose illegal drilling for copper deposits in the Snowdonia National Park.

He won support for his candidature for a place on the new Exmoor Committee from the Ramblers' Association and the Countryside Commission and in August 1973 was appointed, despite his Communist Party background, by the Conservative government headed by Edward Heath.

His account of the first meeting of the new single National Park Committee following the restructuring of the previous tripartite system makes instructive reading, even allowing for his political bias:

> Ten of the other committee members were landowners and another two were personally or professionally associated with the landowning interest. Of the seven members appointed by the Secretary of State for the Environment, to "look after the national interest in conservation and recreation", three were farmers and landowners. Two of them were active members of the Country Landowners Association (CLA) and the third represented Exmoor Hill Farmers at the annual conference of the National Farmers' Union (NFU).

Conflict: The Exmoor House Incident
In 1974 the structure of Exmoor National Park administration changed for the first time since the body was created. Staff from both County Councils came together under the new concept of a National Park Officer, at a new headquarters, Exmoor House, in Dulverton. The Exmoor Society acknowledged that, in terms of administration, this was an improvement. But as Victor Bonham-Carter recorded, the change "did nothing to loosen the hold of the landed interest on the Exmoor National Park Committee, or alter the Authority's policy towards the conservation of moorland."

The new National Park Officer, Ronald Dare Wilson, a retired Major-General with a distinguished military career, had degrees in economics and land economy, a farm near Dulverton, and gave stronger leadership than had been the case under the old arrangements. Nevertheless, as subsequent events were to prove, the new regime was, in the eyes of the Exmoor Society, even more intractable than ever.

What followed proved to be the nadir of the relationship between the Park Authority and the Society. In June 1976, members of the Authority, press representatives and interested members of the public, including Exmoor Society Chairman, Guy Somerset, arrived at Exmoor House for a meeting to discuss a new government requirement: a statutory and formalised National Park Plan for Exmoor. Before the debate the Chairman of the Authority, Major T.F. Trollope-Bellew, announced that press and public would be

Chapter Four: Defending the Fragile Moorland

As he had anticipated whilst lobbying for membership of the Park administration, MacEwen was usually in a minority of one at Exmoor House. He was an isolated figure, generally disliked by his fellow members. Now no longer members of the administration, Bonham-Carter and Burton found themselves in a better position to publicly voice the grave doubts both held regarding the effectiveness of that body. Neither had been impressed with the original governance arrangements for Exmoor and they failed to see much improvement in the new mid-1970s structure which they condemned as "a serious mistake", arguing vehemently that it still denied the administration significant legal powers and funding.

Bonham-Carter wrote in the *Exmoor Review*: "Apart from routine planning matters, the re-structure still left the Park governing body powerless to deal effectively with the main issues that bedevilled Exmoor for many years – in short, those associated with land use." The stage was set, and the protagonists were in place, for years of conflict.

excluded from the proceedings. This was immediately challenged by Guy Somerset, who told him: "You are required to state specifically the reasons why the public are excluded. Will you please do so? You are out of order."

The *West Somerset Free Press* reported Trollope-Bellew's response: "I will not give you one second. I do not want to have to put the full course of the law in operation but, if you do not leave, steps will have to be taken to make you leave." Dare Wilson left the meeting room to fetch police officers to eject the Society Chairman. Before this could happen, the media and Guy Somerset left the building voluntarily, "it being considered preferable to police ejection".

Malcolm MacEwen, at the meeting as a ministerial appointment to the Authority, criticised the secrecy surrounding the Plan, saying: "We should not allow ourselves to become obsessed with the mania for secrecy now affecting local government." Guy Somerset later had harsh words for the Authority and its officers, saying: "It is a National Park Committee, not the Somerset mafia. The public is entitled to know the reasons for decisions, rather than being simply presented with a *fait accompli*."

From a later perspective the incident seems incredible. It was followed by weeks of recrimination and claims that the Committee had acted illegally in excluding press and public. The passions aroused by the conflict are, understandably, difficult to detect in the dry language of official reports and similar documents, but the emotions involved were made quite clear in both press reports and published letters.

The Moorland Loss

Throughout the 1960s and 1970s, Bonham-Carter, Burton, MacEwen and others argued that it was no exaggeration to contend that virtually all that stood in the way of a loss of moorland on a scale that would make a mockery of the area's designation as a National Park was the Exmoor Society. At the head of the threats to the landscape was the issue of reclaiming land through extensive ploughing, a policy which would bring in its wake significant loss of flora and fauna and greatly diminish the scenic appeal which had been an important factor in winning National Park status for Exmoor.

There had been a brief lull in reclamation activity immediately after The Chains victory, which allowed time for the formation of the Society and for it to build up its membership. This human resource was soon discovered to include men and women of varied talents and, just as important, a belief in their cause and a dogged determination which enabled them to fight what at times appeared to be a hopeless battle against indifferent and even openly hostile forces.

Bonham-Carter recorded that business had been slow at first for the Society in its role as watchdog, explaining: "Farmers were too busy, with the aid of government grants, restoring their existing land and livestock after the exertion of the Second World War. In addition, another issue that was to preoccupy the Society over the years was also more or less moribund in 1959. Tourism at the time was regarded as nothing more than a useful cash crop for farmers and others willing to offer accommodation to visitors."

In the years that immediately followed the Second World War, no inroads of consequence had been made into the moorland by farmers, preoccupied with getting back on their feet after the years of war. Exmoor hill farmers at this period were helped by the Livestock Rearing Act and other aid from government, such as guaranteed prices. In complete contrast to the post-1914-18 period, when agriculture was more or less abandoned by government, farming in the late 1940s, 1950s and even later was regarded as a national asset, an essential element in a hard-pressed national economy.

This policy nevertheless generated difficulties not foreseen by conservationists when the National Parks Act became law in 1949. The principal objectives of the Act were to preserve and enhance natural beauty, guard wildlife and make the areas with National Park boundaries available, with reasonable restraints, for public enjoyment, and to do this with "due regard to the needs of farming and forestry".

The clauses within the legislation were well intentioned but the problem for the conservationists began when what had been regarded as the primary objective of the 1949 Act – i.e. the issues of landscape protection and access

Prayway Head, close to the source of the River Exe, looking towards Warren Farm. (Matt Sully/ENPA)

to the countryside – began to play second fiddle to the needs of farming and forestry. This, in the view of Victor Bonham-Carter and those of like mind, was a reversal of the priorities intended by the architects of the legislation.

According to the conservationists, landowners and tenant farmers began, perhaps not surprisingly, to take full advantage of the situation. When the ploughing of conspicuous areas of moorland began to gather real pace, in the years between 1960 and 1965, the Exmoor Society was fairly well established and in a position to mount opposition. The situation led even the Exmoor National Park Committee to become more and more conscious of the weakness of its position and the body asked the Minister of Housing and Local Government (the predecessor to the Department of the Environment) for the legislation to be amended so as to belatedly put some teeth into the 1949 Act.

Exmoor ponies. (Nigel Stone/ENPA)

Recalling the period many years later in *The Essence of Exmoor*, Victor Bonham-Carter regretted the fact that the approach to the Minister was to no avail:

> During this time several thousand acres of heather and grass moorland were lost to the plough and to fencing in areas such as Countisbury, Fyldon Ridge, Porlock Common and Porlock Allotment, all areas valuable for their flora, birds and mammals, and enjoyed by walkers and riders. The Minister took no action because food protection was still the priority policy, dictated by the Ministry of Agriculture, and willingly supported by farmers and landowners, to whom most of the National Park belonged ... who asserted, with some justification, that they had the right to "do what they liked" with their own acres, particularly if reclaiming moorland added to their income.

The 1949 legislation was ambiguous and allowed the government to oppose the proposal, advanced by the Exmoor Society and others, that as the Act was designed primarily to benefit the landscape, wildlife and access, a farmer should be compensated for not ploughing or otherwise altering the sward on his property. In Bonham-Carter's opinion: "By doing nothing Whitehall simply left it to those on the spot to fight it out: which is what happened without reaching a solution, but generating long and bitter controversy."

The afforestation threat to The Chains in 1958 had united people of varying interests and backgrounds. The issue of land reclamation and government unwillingness to intervene had the opposite effect, polarising opinion – those supporting the right to cultivate and those who believed in a duty to conserve.

The result of this seeming impasse was the long period of conflict dubbed by Malcolm MacEwen as "the years of frustration" and remembered today by early Society member Mary Chugg as "a truly dreadful time".

Seeking Practical Solutions

In researching this period it becomes clear that one of the greatest virtues of the individuals driving the strategy of the Exmoor Society was their willingness to adopt a positive approach – constantly seeking practical answers to problems rather than simply opposing developments. Coupled with this was a willingness to accept expert advice from any available source, rather than simply relying on an emotional approach to saving the landscape.

The executive committee of the Society came to the conclusion that the obvious first step towards convincing the Park administration and the government of the justice of its case on reclamation was to define the surviving areas on a map, supported by statistics as to the type and extent of the vegetation. In addition, it was felt necessary to take the heat out of the situation by demonstrating how much moorland had been lost since the designation of the National Park in 1954. Armed with this information, the intention was to present the case for preserving essential areas of moorland, based on a reasoned technical case. Perhaps predictably, the National Park Committee at the time remained unconvinced of the need for such a map.

The Society pressed forward nonetheless, and in 1965 Victor Bonham-Carter approached Alice Coleman, an academic from the Geography Department at King's College, University of London, who was the Director of the Second Land Utilisation Survey. Following an earlier pre-war survey led by Sir Dudley Stamp, this follow-up survey was also designed to be a scientific record of land use across the whole of England and Wales, but with the notable addition of providing information on the semi-natural vegetation of mountain, moor, heath, downland and the like – the very same habitats that were the core factors used in defining the National Parks. Bonham-Carter persuaded Miss Coleman of the urgency of the Exmoor case. She then agreed to place the Exmoor National Park area at the head of the Survey's priority fieldwork mapping programmes.

The principal surveyor in the Land Utilisation Survey, responsible for most of the work on Exmoor, was Geoffrey Sinclair, an expert still active within his chosen field today and undoubtedly a figure who ranks alongside the Society's own activists as one of the principal reasons why so much of Exmoor's iconic landscapes survive in the twenty-first century.

The work that Sinclair was charged to undertake was to record on a series of Ordnance Survey maps detail of the types of agriculture, forestry and

Geoffrey Sinclair, 2020. (Philip Dalling)

semi-natural vegetation (moorland) by means of a standard system of colours and symbols. Sinclair had already covered substantial similar areas throughout the country, and went on to map the majority of upland England and Wales. He made a start at once, and presented the Exmoor Land Use Map (in draft form) at the Society's AGM at South Molton in October 1965. After completing the work, he agreed to keep the map up to date for the Society on an annual basis. It was then loaned to the National Parks Commission in London, shown to the planning staffs of both Somerset and Devon County Councils and to an informal gathering of the National Park Committees of both authorities, who were all enthusiastic and positive once they had seen it in the flesh.

Sinclair extracted a great variety of statistics from the evidence on the map. He divided the National Park into five moorland regions which are still recognised as part of Exmoor's standard landscape typology and have very distinctive visual and ecological qualities. They range from the coastal heather heaths, to the northern and southern heather moors – mainly Common land – which in a horseshoe shape surround the grass moors of the centre where *Molinia* characterises the upper parts of the former royal hunting forest of Exmoor. The latter zone contained 13,800 acres of grass moorland, while the heather moorland, associated heaths, gorse and bracken extended to 36,865 acres. This meant that 50,665 acres (30 per cent of the National Park) remained as the area's core characteristic semi-natural vegetation at the date of survey in 1965.

Using the most recent OS map which showed such "rough grazings" in a simplified form, he calculated that they had covered 58,745 acres in 1957-58. This revealed a loss of more than 8,000 acres or an average of over 1,000 acres a year – mostly to agricultural use and the rest to forestry. Worse was to follow; by June 1966 the total had fallen below 50,000 acres, and the losses continued as the decade progressed, monitored by Sinclair's annual revisions for the Society.

These figures, and Sinclair's detailed analysis of the findings, were published by the Society in 1966 as a game-changing pamphlet, *Can Exmoor Survive?* In addition to the statistics, the document projected the Exmoor Society's view that there was a pressing need to keep the moorland in good heart by means of the traditional system of sheep and cattle grazing. If this system failed, the ground would revert to scrub. The pamphlet also emphasised the extremely delicate balance of vegetation, woodland, and scenery in an area – just 170,000 acres – as small as Exmoor National Park.

Tim Burton, as usual, found exactly the right words to explain to the layman the complex points the Society was making in *Can Exmoor Survive?* when he wrote: "Not only is Exmoor small and fragmented, it is hybrid. By that I mean it consists of various types of scenery: wooded valleys; bare combes; little waters; grass plateaux; heather stretches; a stupendous coast … It is … a delicate patchwork of wildness and cultivation constituting a delicate balance that is easily upset." Burton was deeply critical of the National Park Authority which, he said, had "shown itself insensitive to this fragile beauty". Time and again "it has reacted complacently to a succession of ploughing proposals [by saying] 'After all, it's only a hundred acres' or 'it's an extension of existing improvements'."

By enlisting the aid of disinterested experts, the Exmoor Society had shown a determination to be positive in its approach and back up its claims with the best available scientific evidence.

The Land Use Map and its associated data were completed in time to be presented at the National Parks Conference which was held at Lynton in September 1966 and which brought together representatives of all ten Parks. Sinclair and officers of the Society attended as invited guests. Perhaps predictably, given the climate of the times, the arguments put forward by the Society and the supporting statistics were dismissed out of hand by the Country Landowners' Association and the National Farmers' Union. The two bodies rejected the Society figure of an average of 1,000 acres of moorland lost a year, claiming that the actual figure was less than 100 acres. The NFU and the CLA re-asserted the right of farmers to continue ploughing or otherwise improving the moorland areas as they thought fit.

Building Consensus

On this occasion, however, the Society was not a lone voice crying in the wilderness. At the same conference, representatives of what was then the Ministry of Agriculture, Fisheries and Food (MAFF) and officers of both Somerset and Devon County Councils accepted that Sinclair's figures on moorland loss were correct to within plus or minus three per cent.

The County Council officers subsequently produced their own map, based on Sinclair's, showing what they considered to be moorland "critical to amenity". This showed an area running west from Dunkery Beacon to Chapman Barrows and then south-east to the villages of East and West Anstey, plus some other smaller areas. Crucially, the Council officers not only accepted Sinclair's figures relating to the acreage of surviving moorland but pared it down even further to a critical core of 43,657 acres.

The National Park's Joint Advisory Committee was the next to make a move, insisting in a dramatic letter that unless it was given powers to control the ploughing and fencing of moorland, the government should repeal the provisions of the 1949 Act which required National Parks to preserve and enhance the landscape and thus relieve them of the burden of conserving it. An opportunity for government to take such action was not long in presenting itself, in the form of the 1968 Countryside Act. To the great disappointment of the Society, this was largely wasted, with the new legislation simply requiring farmers to give six months' notice of their intention to plough within the "critical amenity" area prescribed by the Somerset and Devon County Council officers. No compensation was offered for not ploughing and, should negotiations with the farmers involved fail, the National Park Authority possessed no sanction.

With compulsory purchase of threatened moorland areas vetoed by the government, the 1968 Act was viewed by Bonham-Carter, speaking for the Society, as "a failure". Sinclair had agreed to revise the map on an annual basis for the Society by recording changes affecting the extent of the moorland. The findings were published in *The Vegetation of Exmoor* (Exmoor Press, 1970) which provided more detail of the mapping work and the botanical content of the vegetation, but also documented a longer-term analysis of moorland change from the earlier Ordnance Survey in 1913 and the First Land Use Survey in 1934. Sinclair's annual revisions post 1965 to 1969 demonstrated a continued but tapering reduction, but one which showed that the problem had not yet been solved.

Economic problems meant that the early 1970s saw a lull in the land reclamation dispute, raising hopes that no further Exmoor moorland would be lost. These hopes were shattered when, in 1976, plans were submitted for the ploughing up of two areas of moorland in a highly sensitive place close to the Bristol Channel coast, on either side of the main A39 road linking Lynton and Lynmouth and Porlock, adjacent to the area where the issue had first raised itself some ten years earlier.

The land involved in the new proposals was 250 acres at Yenworthy and North Common and 375 acres at Stowey Allotment. The land at North Common was spared the plough by its owner, Ben Halliday, a schoolmaster who had unexpectedly inherited the large Glenthorne Estate. The National Park Committee was interested in buying Stowey Allotment, but in the event was outbid by a young farmer, who immediately declared his intention to plough most if it, under the six months' notice agreement.

Not long before the notice was due to expire, the Countryside Commission intervened, made the matter public and offered to pay nearly ninety per cent of the cost of a year-long management agreement, which would allow time for reconsideration of the matter. The National Park Authority declined the offer and, in Bonham-Carter's words, "another valuable section of the heartland of the moor was lost". A loss indeed, but one that aroused considerable indignation in many circles and proved to be a major turning point in the struggle against the disappearance of moorland.

The Countryside Commission made its feelings plain to Whitehall and a deputation from Somerset County Council visited Dennis Howell, Minister of State at the Department of the Environment, urging him to intervene. Malcolm MacEwen, so often a lone voice urging conservation within the Exmoor National Park Committee, had already made his own representations to Howell.

The Porchester Inquiry
The urgings of the Countryside Commission, Somerset councillors and MacEwen, an increasingly influential figure within the wider conservation movement, brought a rich reward. For the first time joint action was taken by the Ministry of Agriculture, Food and Fisheries and the Department of the Environment. Lord Porchester (later the Earl of Carnarvon) was appointed to conduct an inquiry into the whole issue of land use and reclamation.

MacEwen initially had his doubts about the inquiry. Porchester was a landowner, with family connections at Pixton Park, on the edge of Exmoor. On the credit side, he was a much-respected former Chairman of the County Councils Association. Any such doubts, whether harboured by MacEwen or other Society members, evaporated as the Conservative Peer got down to work.

Bonham-Carter summed up the feelings of the Society as the inquiry began its hearings by saying: "In short, Porchester carried great authority, and this became increasingly evident in the thorough manner in which he and his aides assembled the facts, conducted interviews and arranged meetings with all interested parties ... He was a rigorous interrogator and spared no group or individual with his searching questions."

Lord Porchester spent most of the summer of 1977 pursuing his brief from the government, exploring Exmoor, studying maps and reading the copious literature that arrived constantly on his desk, which included the Exmoor Society's pamphlet *Can Exmoor Survive?* He spent a day touring the moor with its author Geoffrey Sinclair, a fruitful dialogue only marred by the descent of typical Exmoor clouds, but in oral evidence to the inquiry Sinclair submitted that it should never be forgotten that farmers must have an appropriate but continuing management role as they were "the key part of the ecology of Exmoor". Porchester's Report, *A Study of Exmoor*, was published in November 1977. In the words of Bonham-Carter, "[it] proved a turning point in the whole campaign to save the moorland – although not all its recommendations were accepted and it took several years for the implementation, even of its prime findings, to take effect."

Lord Porchester's team on Exmoor. Lord Porchester is the second from the right. On the far right is Jim Collins, Exmoor National Park's first ranger. (ENPA)

A Study of Exmoor was a very comprehensive document, with thirteen chapters. Bonham-Carter's assessment, written from the Society's perspective, highlighted the salient points. Essentially, said Bonham-Carter, Porchester had identified the central issue, of "the conflict between increased agricultural production from moorland and the need to maintain the existing balance of the Exmoor landscape".

MAFF had been giving grants for agricultural "improvement" in sensitive areas without reference to conservation, thereby undermining the basic aims of the 1949 National Parks Act. The Porchester Report accepted the importance of the vegetation types classified by Sinclair in *Can Exmoor Survive?* and *The Vegetation of Exmoor*, which recorded the loss of 8,000 acres of moorland between 1957 and 1969. Using aerial photography, Porchester subsequently confirmed that in the extended period between 1947 and 1977 as much as 12,000 acres had been lost – 9,500 to agriculture and 2,500 to forestry.

Porchester concluded that officials considering applications from farmers for grants to convert moorland into productive agricultural land must take into account the interests of the environment at an early stage. It was not valid in the Exmoor context to argue that a grant application was confidential. The Report described the term "critical amenity" as being inadequate and urged that a category of land needed to be established in which change must be utterly resisted. All moorland, wherever located in the National Park, must be treated as sensitive.

The essential areas of Exmoor as defined by Porchester included what was generally described by the Society as "the heartland" – the tract of moorland from Dunkery Beacon in the east to Chapman Barrows in the west, including the northern heather moors and the contiguous portion of the central grass moors, together with the coastal heathland, the southern heather moors and other isolated areas of exceptional ecological or scenic value.

Porchester's findings indicated a preference for the protection of moorland by voluntary action wherever possible, in the interests of good relations between the individuals and bodies concerned. This, he believed, could be achieved by the National Park Committee purchasing the land involved outright, or by securing management agreements with adequate rates of compensation for the landowners/farmers.

The Report recommended the adoption of a Moorland Conservation Order (MCO) "to prevent such operations and practices as are likely to alter the vegetation or the general character of the moorland to any material degree". The MCO would also serve to secure public access to moorland in appropriate cases.

The Porchester Report included two maps – the first identifying all the areas of Exmoor predominantly formed of moorland or heath. This was intended to be a catalogue, not a statement of policy. The purpose of the second map was to define those particular tracts of land whose traditional appearance would be considered by the National Park Committee as necessary "to conserve for all time" from agricultural or silvicultural (the cultivation of forest trees) conversion.

The final part of the Report dealt with the likely cost of Porchester's recommendations. The conservation of all the areas defined in the second map would, over a period of years, amount to £750,000 at 1977 values, this sum to be provided by the Treasury.

The Exmoor National Park Committee accepted the Porchester Report, its reservations mainly confined to the issue of compensation, a concern soon ironed out. To a certain degree, politics then intervened. The provision for compulsory Moorland Conservation Orders was duly incorporated in the Countryside Bill of 1979, drafted for James Callaghan's incumbent Labour government, which at the time was surviving only with support from the Liberal Party. The Act failed to reach the Statute Book – it required just six more hours of debate to go through Parliament when Callaghan lost a vote of confidence in the House. The subsequent General Election was won by Margaret Thatcher and the Conservative Party.

The powers recommended by Porchester would have incorporated the Statutory Compensation Code of "before and after" capital values. Land values on Exmoor bear little relation to its productive capacity and resorting to the Moorland Conservation Orders, or even their existence as a backstop, would have prevented proper compensation to the already disadvantaged upland farmers. They would be penalised for having maintained moorland areas while seeing others obtaining additional income from improved pastures and thereby keeping their young people engaged in agriculture where they had been brought up.

On Exmoor, following the Porchester Report, management agreements were successfully negotiated on the basis of profits forgone and the formula for this radical departure from the Statutory Compensation Code was incorporated by the new Conservative government into its own Wildlife and Countryside Act 1981. From the Exmoor management agreements sprang the whole raft of agri-environmental schemes – and an acceptance that public money should be used for positive land-management practices as well as restrictions.

Management Agreements and Section Three Maps

Despite the 1979 change to the political landscape, the two maps produced by Porchester were completed and subsequently given the single title of the Conservation Map. Eventually, in the 1985 Wildlife and Countryside Act, it became a statutory duty for all National Parks to produce such documents, known as Section Three Maps, showing areas to be conserved for all time and including mountain, moor, heath, woodland, down, cliff and foreshore.

The total area of Exmoor under protection would be just under 40,000 acres, later extended by the designation of Sites of Special Scientific Interest (SSSIs) and Nature Reserves (NRs).

Although the incoming Conservative government had rejected the Porchester proposal for MCOs in its Wildlife and Countryside Act, the administration agreed that the Treasury should meet ninety per cent of the total cost of management agreements – a major plank of Porchester's findings. The actual sum involved in a management agreement was to be calculated by the Agricultural Economics Unit at the University of Exeter.

Although not a panacea for all the ills confronting Exmoor, the value of the Porchester Report to the wellbeing of the National Park landscape was immense. The role the Exmoor Society had played in creating the climate which paved the way for Porchester could also not be underestimated. In his inimitable way, Bonham-Carter summed it up succinctly:

> If it had not been for the 20-year campaign waged by the Exmoor Society in the 1960s and 1970s, no Porchester Report would have been commissioned or published and no legislation enacted.

> If allowed to continue unchecked, ploughing and fencing of the privately owned areas of the moorland would have deprived Exmoor of its special character, and its claim to the status of a National Park. Porchester was a breakthrough that never would have occurred without the persistent efforts of a handful of individuals (and their relatively few supporters) putting their hands in their pockets and lobbying tirelessly for the cause. It was a truly democratic phenomenon.

In his later years Bonham-Carter became progressively disabled and was unable to continue his regular visits to the Exmoor Society's headquarters. He nevertheless continued to take a close interest in the affairs of the Society he had served so well and in 1995, looking back over forty years of the Exmoor National Park, recalled not only the impact of the Porchester Report but also the changes for the better that had been made possible by the progressive restructuring of the governing body of Exmoor National Park.

The 1993 Annual General Meeting of the Exmoor Society. The group includes no fewer than three chairmen of the Society. Back row from left to right: *Frank Suter, a trustee, Michael Hawkins (former Chairman), Jim Thompson, Bishop of Bath and Wells (a Vice-President), Guy Somerset (Chairman);* front row: *Victor Bonham-Carter (former Chairman) and Sally Thompson.* (Exmoor Society Archive)

The Society had cautiously welcomed the 1974 simplification of the administrative structure, while regretting that the changes still left the body well short of the teeth it required to control issues such as land use. By 1999 the National Park Committee had achieved independence within the local government system and become the National Park Authority. This, said Bonham-Carter, enabled the body to administer Exmoor effectively, although he added: "This in no way lessens the importance of the role played by the Society as a watchdog and as an innovator."

Reconciliation

Victor Bonham-Carter died in March 2007, a couple of years short of the Society's golden jubilee. His prediction that the organisation would continue to be needed to fight in the interests of Exmoor has been vindicated time and time again. But, at the end of his life, he was at least able to be content that the seemingly endless years of struggle, when even the most optimistic activists feared for the very continuing existence of Exmoor in any recognisable form, had ended. A flavour of the depth of the bitterness that

Chapter Four: Defending the Fragile Moorland

previously existed is contained in the account of the Exmoor House incident of 1976, which can be found on pages 36-37.

The exact point at which that era of bitterness in the relations between the conservationists, represented chiefly by the Exmoor Society, the landowning interest and the National Park administration and other bodies, was replaced by a more cordial atmosphere is difficult to pinpoint with any great precision. And, from its own point of view, the Society still jealously guards its role as a watchdog, acting in the public interest where Exmoor is concerned.

But a good contender for the acknowledgment on all sides of the need for reconciliation and co-operation would be Saturday 20 May 1989, a brilliant sunny day on which the Society celebrated its thirtieth anniversary with a rally at what was by then the Pinkery Farm Exploration Centre, close to the area of The Chains threatened all those years before by afforestation.

On the day some sixty people gathered at Pinkery, for an event which was to prove much more than a simple birthday party. It brought together a wide range of individuals and organisations with interests in the National Park, people who undoubtedly shared a love of, and a concern for, the wellbeing of Exmoor, but whose varying beliefs and priorities had for three decades produced an atmosphere of often harsh conflict. That day at Pinkery and the subsequent walk across The Chains with Society members, representatives of the National Park, the Forestry Commission and other organisations with a vested interest in the moor, went a long way towards drawing a line underneath the difficulties and disagreements that had gone before.

Victor Bonham-Carter, by now President of the Society he had helped to nurture, and one of the principal players on the Society side during the years of conflict, hit the right note at the start of The Chains Rally when he welcomed the assembly. He reviewed the events of the first three decades of the Society's history, during which time it had "fought a vigorous, persistent, usually unpopular campaign to save the moorland, then being ploughed and enclosed by farmers, who were receiving grants to boost food production."

> They were of course within their rights to do so, but it made nonsense of the prime purpose of the National Parks Act 1949 – namely to conserve specific areas of great landscape beauty and ecological value and to allow public access for enjoyment. In essence the Government of the day had not thought the matter through – the Act was ambivalent – and had left it to the people on the spot to fight it out. Hence the fierce arguments deployed by both sides, a lot of bad feeling, and the assumption that the Exmoor Society was a bunch of up-country outsiders interfering in other people's business.

SAVING THE SPLENDOUR: *The History of the Exmoor Society*

Here: *Walk across The Chains after the party at Pinkery.*
Below: *Lady Arran planting an ash tree at Pinkery on the occasion of the Chains Rally in 1989, helped by Gwyn Francis, Director General of the Forestry Commission, and David Wood, a forester.*
(Both photos Shipsey/Exmoor Society Archive)

He went on to say: "All these troubles are past history. No bitterness today, but a feeling of reconciliation and an entirely new attitude to the natural environment."

In an act Bonham-Carter described as being of great symbolic importance, Lady Arran, granddaughter of Lord Fortescue, the landowner of The Chains, planted several broad-leaved trees at the Pinkery site. The trees were a gift from the Forestry Commission, the body which in 1958 had intended to buy The Chains from the Fortescue family and plant conifers on the plateau. Victor Bonham-Carter continued:

> The very fact that we have asked Lady Arran … and that she has kindly accepted our invitation to plant a group of broad-leaved trees here … is a symbol of our common understanding and indeed of all of us who have the interests of the National Park at heart – landowners, farmers, conservationists, riders, ramblers, whoever. We all want hill farmers on Exmoor, especially family farmers, to survive and be given Government support to do so as an integral part of conservational husbandry, which is traditional husbandry based on sheep and beef; and in that and other practical and financial ways to restore and enhance the landscape of the National Park.

The National Parks movement was represented at the gathering by Michael Dower, National Park Officer for the first National Park to be created, the Peak District, and Chairman of the Association of National Park Officers. Dower was the son of John Dower, a former Secretary of the Standing Committee on National Parks, whose 1945 Report to the Attlee government of the day was so influential in the creation of Britain's Parks (see Chapter One).

Michael Dower told those present at Pinkery that the National Parks movement as a whole had reason to be doubly grateful to the Exmoor Society:

> The saving of The Chains from afforestation … was important not only because it kept open the high heartland of Exmoor … but also because it focussed attention on the need to reconcile (on the one hand) the interests of landowners and (on the other) the national concern to protect the landscape and to provide access to the hills. [The Society's fight to conserve moorland] laid the groundwork for today's greater (but still fragile) stability in the state of Exmoor's moorland. It also led directly to the nationwide system (under the Wildlife and Countryside Act 1981) whereby National Park Authorities can influence what landowners do with their land.

Gwyn Francis, Director-General of the Forestry Commission, continued the theme of reconciliation first developed at the event by Bonham-Carter, saying:

> With past conflict behind us, we are now able to discuss the issues and policies, the aims and objectives of our respective organisations with mutual respect and deeper understanding ... I am [also] pleased to be here because it gives me an opportunity to emphasise the Forestry Commission's obligation under the Wildlife and Countryside Act to endeavour to achieve a balance between the needs of timber production with those of the environment.

Keith Bungay, at the time of the 1989 Chains Rally approaching the end of his first year as Exmoor's National Parks Officer, recalled his first contact with the Exmoor Society when its representatives visited Exmoor House:

> Present on that day were names that even those who had previously lived well away from Exmoor knew so well – Guy Somerset, Malcolm MacEwen and Victor Bonham-Carter. It was rather like one of those greasy poles at a village fête where an innate instability, coupled with forceful blows coming from all directions, generates an extreme sense of vulnerability. I survived – just – principally, I would suggest, because of the courtesy and kindness of my guests from the Society ...

> The basic concept of conserving the special landscapes of the National Parks for the enjoyment of the public at large still holds good. The work, enthusiasm and dedication of voluntary bodies like the Exmoor Society is central to that concept.

No one within the Society present at the 1989 Chains Rally doubted that there were continuing and new struggles ahead. Rachel Thomas, attending the Rally as a former member of the Exmoor National Park Authority and a Countryside Commissioner, spoke of the unique opportunity new legislation and new attitudes had created for National Parks to guide change, restore habitats and to create new landscapes for the future. "All this does mean a different approach from us all and new opportunities for the Exmoor Society. There are so many challenges ahead and the National Park community must be ready to face the future."

In subsequent years, the Society's ground-breaking *Moorland Report* of 2004 and the 2016 update of the *Exmoor's Moorland: Where Next?* study made important steps towards meeting these challenges.

Chapter Five
Supporting Upland Farmers

"Farmers are naturally suspicious about amenity societies such as ours ... too many think we want to sterilise Exmoor ... We cannot honestly deny that our interests do sometimes conflict ... [but] we welcome a prosperous agriculture on the moor."

Exmoor Review, 1961

After reading the preceding chapter about the battles to prevent what many saw as the likely out-and-out destruction of Exmoor's wild moorland, it would be all too easy to believe the attitude to the farming community which prevailed within the Exmoor Society during its early years was one of misunderstanding at best and outright hostility at worst.

Nothing could be further from the truth. Although the more radical conservationists within the Society, often from an urban background, were always likely to sit uneasily alongside the landowners and the hill farmers, a very strong element within the Society membership always sought to understand the position of those who earned a living from the moor and sympathised with their many difficulties.

Very early in the Society's existence an article in the 1961 *Exmoor Review* set out exactly where the organisation stood in relation to agriculture. The piece was credited to "the officers of the Society" but it bears the hallmarks of the style of the Society's founding father and first Chairman, John Coleman-Cooke.

The article acknowledged at the outset that the relationship between the Exmoor farming community and the Society was likely to be on occasions a difficult one. Exploring that relationship, the writers did not pull any punches, stating:

> Only experts – or fools – or politicians – try to lay down the law about agriculture. Farmers are naturally suspicious about amenity societies such as ours; too many think that we are against any kind of agricultural development, that we want to sterilise Exmoor, that we prefer old-fashioned methods and buildings, that we grudge every new acre won from the moor, that the tripper should come before the stock-breeder, that we prefer pests to poisons and that we want quaintness rather than progress. We cannot honestly deny that our interests do sometimes conflict. Let us be frank, we prefer the old-fashioned village to the

> dormitory town, the rural countryside to the intensive market garden, the open moor to the fenced-in, ploughed-up ley.
>
> We deplore, for instance, the blemish along Weir Water. In these beauty spots surely the interests of amenity should have had priority over costly agricultural development? On the other hand we admire the pioneering spirit of the farmers who have reclaimed land that has more agricultural than amenity value.

The authors of the article placed a great deal of responsibility for the acceptable management of the moor upon the shoulders of the officials of the then Ministry of Agriculture responsible for administering the improvement schemes which were such a controversial topic on Exmoor. Reclamation, according to the Society, needed not only to be worthwhile from the agricultural and financial point of view – and the Society believed this aspect to be marginal in many of the schemes submitted – but the effect on amenity in a National Park had also to be considered.

Summing up the Society's attitude towards the farming community, the writers concluded by stating firmly that the two groups "must learn to live with one another", adding:

> The rolling, open moor is not only picturesque; it provides healthy grazing for cattle and sheep, and it is an attraction for thousands of tourists and sportsmen. But farmers must live, and to live well these days they must be efficient. We welcome a prosperous agriculture on Exmoor; there is no joy, or money, in derelict farmsteads and weed-ridden pastures; there is delight, and money, in a tidy farm and healthy stock.

Warren Farm, one of the most remote farms on Exmoor. (ENPA)

> We have published, and will continue to publish, articles by farmers and agricultural experts in an attempt to explain the nature and problems of Exmoor agriculture to the layman … Much of the distrust is caused by ignorance, and it is this ignorance, perhaps on both sides, that we want to dispel.

The Society was not, of course, about to abandon its concerns over land use and reclamation, and afforestation.

A lighter touch, yet with an underlying seriousness, was provided by a goodwill message from the Devon author Henry Williamson, of *Tarka the Otter* fame, published in the 1962 *Review*. Williamson, who held office as a Vice-President of the Society, supported its aim to keep Exmoor as Exmoor, commenting: "We know that trees must be planted to conserve rainfall and thereby the soil; but we don't want all of the moor to look like Carver Doone's beard seen through a telescope from Dartmoor, and vice-versa."

Enabling the Debate

The promise to publish articles on farming was faithfully kept by the editors of the *Review*, even when much of the content might be at odds with the views held by the Society. Regular contributor E.R. "Dick" Lloyd wrote at some length on the subject of modern hill farming in the context of the second half of the twentieth century and as seen in the light of the 1947 Hill Farming Act. It was a topic he was well qualified to tackle, as manager of the Honeymead Estate near Simonsbath, owned, since 1927, by the Waley-Cohen family, who had purchased it from the Fortescues.

Much carping criticism, Dick Lloyd said, had been heard about the "feather bedding effect" for the hill-farming communities of subsidies and grants. But this legislation, he insisted, had allowed many thousands of acres of potentially productive land which had slipped further and further back towards their primeval state of bog, gorse and heather to return to the healthy state in which they had existed before the 1914-18 war. Lloyd continued:

> Nevertheless, if in the public interest hill farms are to be kept reasonably productive and capable of expansion in times of national crisis, some measure of special assistance is bound to be maintained, not only for sound capital improvements, but also for revenue maintenance, otherwise the hill farms will become so uneconomic and unattractive financially … that no one will be found to farm them … the hill farmer must, in the national interest, be treated exceptionally to the rest of the industry in this matter of capital grants and subsidies for agriculture.

Tom Robins, the Emperor of Exmoor

Over the years the *Exmoor Review*, whilst reflecting the Society's interest in the variety of policy issues concerning the farming community of the National Park, never lost sight of the human angle and the many great characters whose closeness to the land brought them a deep knowledge of the moor.

The subject chosen for the *Review's* very first profile of a farming personality in 1959 was Tom Robins, known affectionately as "the Emperor of Exmoor". His working life began at the age of twelve, on his father's farm at Grattan Barton, in Bratton Fleming; he later moved to South Lydcote, where he was proud to be known as a hill farmer for the rest of his days, preferring to raise Red Devon cattle and Exmoor Horn sheep, because they were native to the county and to the moor.

Tom Robins by R.L. Knight. (North Devon Athenaeum and the *North Devon Journal*)

He was active for most of his life in national agricultural circles and moorland farmers owed him a debt of gratitude. When the Blackmoor Gate branch of the NFU met to discuss farming policy in wartime, and the encouragement of beef and cattle rearing instead of the selling off of the calves for veal, Tom Robins declared: "Cash will encourage the hill farmer, or any farmer".

A resolution to that effect went to London and from the Ministry of Agriculture and Fisheries came the cash encouragement to rear beef – a policy which continued for many years. He served as hill farming representative of the NFU in London and received the MBE. He was active in his local community, serving as treasurer when the new Methodist Chapel at Brayford was built, and was a stalwart of Charles and High Bray Flower Show. He hunted with the Devon and Somerset Staghounds and was a great supporter of local traditions. He read widely and wrote a little himself on moorland subjects. It was due to him that the Sloley Stone, north of Mole's Chamber on the boundary of the old Forest of Exmoor, was re-erected after it had fallen down.

The recognition and encouragement of individuals such as Tom Robins, and the many other Exmoor personalities who have appeared over the years in the columns of the *Review*, is a cherished policy of the Society, summed up in the website declaration of support for life on Exmoor and on the upland family farms that play a crucial role in maintaining and enhancing the assets of the National Park.

Harnessing Expertise

A feature of the Exmoor Society over the decades has been an ability to recognise the vast bank of expertise existing well beyond the boundaries of West Somerset and North Devon and a willingness to recruit that expertise to further the cause of conserving the National Park. Chapter Four highlighted the major role played by Geoffrey Sinclair, who at the time of his greatest involvement with Exmoor was Chief Field Officer of the Second Land Use Survey of Great Britain and the man responsible for the Land Use Map of Exmoor commissioned by the Exmoor Society.

In the 1969 *Exmoor Review* Sinclair addressed some of the issues concerning hill farming in an article entitled 'Fair Play and Fair Pay in National Parks'. Britain, he wrote, was so short of space that in cases where land could serve more than one purpose, it should be allowed to do so.

> That is the meaning of Multiple Use. It applies particularly to National Parks, such as Exmoor, where the land produces food and timber, stores water, is a habitat of wild life (plants and animals), and provides magnificent scenery enjoyed by thousands of visitors every year. But there is a corollary. Multiple Use should be multiply financed. That is, each kind of use should contribute towards its own cost. In the National Parks it is the landowners and farmers who, by owning and maintaining the land, make the enjoyment of scenery possible by the tourist; yet, by and large, it is they who have shared least in the prosperity brought by tourism. True, a number of farmers take in summer visitors, sell cream ... and hire out horses; but these are only fringe activities, not practised by all, nor do they affect the central problem – which is to integrate farming with amenity...

> But one thing is certain. If you break up areas of moorland of 'critical amenity value', i.e. those essential to wild life and/or beautiful scenery typical of the region, then you destroy for ever a heritage which gives life to wild plants and animals (such as the red deer), and which attracts visitors and income. On the other hand, any plan to sterilise moorland by giving up the practice of controlled grazing is just as bad. The land will just deteriorate into woody scrub and benefit nobody. The fact is that amenity and hill grazing are interdependent, the one supporting the other, and until recently the marriage worked well ... economic pressures on farming have brought about the divorce and so long as farm use is differently financed from amenity use the separation will continue. Moreover, unless something positive is done to correct this situation, it is bound to result in the virtual extinction of moorland.

A fascinating contribution to the *Review* on the subject of the Society and farmers was published in 1974, with the eye-catching title 'Should farmers

Sheep auction at Exford in 1972.
(John Tucker/ENPA)

always be Losers?' The author, Mary Tyndale Biscoe, responding to previous articles on the relationship between conservationists and Exmoor farmers, suggested that "the sometimes aggressive determination of some farmers to plough moorland" probably had its roots in "old, unhappy, far-off things". Tyndale Biscoe, an academic, added:

> Farmers, like miners, were under-rated and under-rewarded – except in times of war, and the older ones still have bitter memories of the fearful decay and desolation of farmland between the [First and Second World] wars ... If the farmer is seen, as he must be, as an integral part of Exmoor National Park policy, then he must be allowed to pursue his legitimate farming activities, and not be edged and pressured into becoming either a hotelier, park attendant, or shopkeeper for health foods.

Sheepdog trials at Challacombe. (Philip Dalling)

Quit the Moor Resignations

The remarks included in an early edition of the *Review* acknowledging that the relationship between the Society and Exmoor farmers was difficult, and accepting that the farmers as a class were suspicious of the motives of amenity societies, reflected the position which existed for much of the twentieth century. It is clear that the farmers had good reason to be wary of some Society activists; on the other hand, they also had supporters within the organisation who were willing to go to considerable lengths – including resignation – to plead the farmers' case.

A small group immortalised in the press headline 'Moor Four Quit' consisted of three men and a woman who had joined the executive of the Exmoor Society with the specific aim of trying to mend the fractured relationship between the organisation and the farmers in the National Park. The four were Christopher Thomas-Everard, a landowner, Michael Scott, a dairy farmer, Hazel Eardley-Wilmott, an archaeologist and author of the book *Yesterday's Exmoor*, and Hugh Thomas, land agent for the Fortescue Estate. Their efforts to use their position on the executive to repair the Society–farmer rift ended in disappointment. They became frustrated by the discovery that decisions were being made about Society policy towards farming without discussion in executive meetings.

The atmosphere of the times, despite the protestations of support for upland farmers and claims of an understanding of their difficulties, was very different to that of the present day, as will become obvious, particularly in the final chapter of this book. Today the Exmoor Society recognises the key role of farmers in shaping the landscape, recovering nature, helping mitigate climate change through carbon sequestration, reducing flooding and encouraging visitors and local people to enjoy many different experiences.

As the turn of the century approached the Society worked hard not only to improve its own relationship with the farming community but also to promote a positive image of upland farmers generally, accepting that they were a frequently undervalued section of British agriculture. The Society scored a major success in April 2006 when it brought about a Royal visit to the National Park, with a firm focus on agriculture.

A Royal Visit

The Princess Royal visited several of Exmoor's remotest communities to see at first hand some of the principal issues surrounding rural life. Her first task on the day was to help launch Exmoor National Park's latest Management Plan – *A Sustainable Future for Exmoor* – at Lynton Town Hall. The Plan, compiled after consultation with the Exmoor Society and other interested parties, identified eight areas where concerted action was needed to achieve the best for Exmoor in years to come. These areas were: the future of farming on Exmoor; a changing Exmoor landscape; Exmoor's historic environment; Exmoor's wildlife; tourism and recreation; Exmoor's environment; local people and communities; and understanding and awareness.

In addition to the initiation of this important Management Plan, more than sixty people representing twenty-five different organisations with an interest in Exmoor attended the event and organised displays. After this fairly formal start to the visit, the cavalcade of Range Rovers carrying the Royal party then set off down some of Exmoor's narrowest meandering lanes. The first port of call was Molland, in North Devon, for a visit hosted by the owners of the Molland Estate, Clare and Andrew McLaren Throckmorton. Mrs McLaren Throckmorton said the couple were "thrilled to bits" at the visit.

Princess Anne had visited the estate some twenty-five years previously, for eventing, but the new visit was particularly important because the Royal visitor would be meeting farmers who were suffering through not getting their payments from Defra. The estate owner added: "The government is not behaving well and it's a nightmare to keep this place alive. I inherited the estate from my uncle fifteen years ago and since then I have had a vision of keeping it green and alive."

Princess Anne then moved on to Molland village, where the flag of St George was proudly fluttering from the tower of the church of St Mary, one of Exmoor's gems of ecclesiastical architecture with a Georgian interior thankfully overlooked by Victorian "restorers". Close to the church were gathered many of the tiny community's residents – there were just 156 at the time on the electoral roll. They included Molland's oldest inhabitant, 83-year-old Ralph Lock and his wife Lorna, who sat in chairs holding aloft a banner which proclaimed "God bless our Royal family".

Waiting patiently at the nearby London Inn were twenty local farmers, all keen to air their views. This part of the visit was scheduled to last for an hour, but the Princess Royal's knowledge of farming and her obvious interest in the problems faced by the agricultural community stretched the meeting out to double that time. The discussions focused on the problems caused by the delay in single farm payments, the loss of abattoirs and the difficulty of encouraging young people to take an interest in agriculture. Rachel Thomas said after the visit:

> Many of the points raised by the farmers were included in the Society's report, *Moorlands at a Crossroads*, which revealed that there is a lack of consensus on the future direction the moorland should take. The report

The Princess Royal talking with farmers in the London Inn, Molland, 2006. (Steve Guscott/ENPA)

showed how Molland Moor was an example of some of the wider challenges facing Exmoor's moorland and how issues such as under grazing and scrub encroachment, deterioration in the condition of the landscape and the archaeological resource needed to be dealt with because this heather moorland is nationally important. Hopefully airing the difficulties facing farming will lead to further understanding by government agencies and greater flexibility in the way moorlands generally can be managed by traditional methods that have been used through the centuries.

Princess Anne added a lot to the conversations, being particularly interested in the need to bring young people into farming and how vital it was to keep amenities such as the village shop, which she was able to visit, and places like the superb London Inn. Andrew Hawkins, who farmed one of the highest acreages on the moor, said later: "The Princess Royal was very switched on and understood the problems faced by upland farmers."

The Princess Royal heard some straight talking too. Exford farmer Oliver Edwards was quoted in the *North Devon Journal* as saying: "The trouble is that the suits in London think we're all peasants here. This is a traditional hill farming area. We have learned things over the generations and that is why Exmoor is Exmoor." And Fred Pook, who raised sheep and cattle on Molland Moor, talked to the Royal visitor about the difficulties facing farmers with new Defra regulations. He said: "Our problem is that the moor has now gone back to being like a jungle because we're not allowed to graze it properly."

The Royal visit to Molland in 2006 certainly helped to raise the national profile of the crisis in upland farming. Some eighteen months later, in November 2008, the Society and its sister body the Dartmoor Preservation Association took their case for urgent action right to the heart of government.

The Society Spring Conference of that year had focused on hill farming and among the distinguished guest speakers on that occasion was an Exmoor resident, Society member and now Vice-President, Baroness Ann Mallalieu, who was to become President of the Countryside Alliance. Following the Conference she suggested that a good way to bring the problems of the upland farmer to national prominence would be for the Exmoor Society and the Dartmoor Preservation Association to hold a joint Parliamentary Reception at the House of Lords.

Informing Politics
Baroness Malallieu helped to host the event which was attended by the past and current Ministers of State for Sustainable Food and Farming and Animal Health at the Department for Environment, Food and Rural Affairs, Jeff (later Lord) Rooker and his successor in the post, Huw Irranca-Davies. Rooker, who had been popular in rural circles during his tenure of the post, emphasised the importance of livestock farming in the uplands and the many public benefits it provided. He acknowledged the fears over the survival of hill farming but said the problem would not be overcome solely by public subsidies.

Speaking at the Reception, Society Chairman Rachel Thomas said there was now a growing recognition that there was a problem with hill farming and its economic viability. She added: "People generally do not make the connection between hill-farming practices and environmental and public benefits. This vindicates the approach of the Exmoor Society and the Dartmoor Preservation Association to raise awareness of the significance of the uplands nationally, and the role that hill farming plays."

The Exmoor Society Chairman went on to emphasise that the uplands were not homogenous areas and decision making therefore needed to be devolved locally. There remained disagreement over the ability of the nationally devised environmental schemes, including the controversial Upland Elementary Level Scheme, to work successfully, with a feeling that further adjustments were required. Rachel Thomas concluded that there was considerable scope for both Exmoor and Dartmoor to provide more evidence of the need for the survival of hill farming and the environmental goods and services the sector provided.

It is now recognised that the 2008 Parliamentary Reception had a positive outcome, with the lobbying by the Society and its Dartmoor counterpart, helped by the two National Park authorities, raising the profile of upland farming, and leading to a new income stream for farmers rearing cattle.

Coming closer to the present day and continuing to address the vital issue of upland farming, the Exmoor Society has devoted much time and thought to the consequences of a British exit from the European Union. Following the Referendum decision in 2016 to leave, the Society set about assessing the effect on Exmoor's farmers of life outside the EU. The significance of British membership of the EU and what it was likely to mean to farmers had occupied the Society since the early 1960s, the period when the United Kingdom under the premiership of Harold Macmillan first sought membership of what was then known as the European Economic Community or, more familiarly, as the Common Market.

The Exmoor Society's report to its members in the summer 1962 edition of the *Review* emphasised once again the organisation's inherent support for farming on the moor. The report's section on agriculture said:

> We feel genuine sympathy with the hill farmers, now that the Government appears to them to be blowing cold on agriculture, and with the threat of an even colder east wind from the Continent. No farmer has set out to farm on Exmoor with the sole object of making money; no farmer on Exmoor can make money without measures of Government support; no Exmoor farmer can welcome the principle that he is dependent for his living on government subsidies.

> Farming on Exmoor is a way of life, with most farming families inter-related, and many farms being handed down from generation to generation … Exmoor may be one of the last refuges in this country of the truly independent farmer. He will contrive to stay on his family farm because he loves the land and devotes all his energies to its improvement and the welfare of his stock. Let us hope that as the last of the old estates disintegrate the families who farmed as tenants will not be displaced by agriculturalists with no deep feeling for the history and future of the Moor.

> We have said before that we are in favour of a prosperous farming community. We hope that the agriculture of Exmoor is virile enough to stand on its own feet, [and] strong enough to withstand the competition of the Common Market … We would like to hear more of the sterling qualities of Exmoor sheep and cattle, irrespective of breed. We would like to see more Exmoor lamb and beef described as such in shops, and a vogue for Exmoor wool.

Understanding the economics of farming on Exmoor today. Dr Keith Howe, current Vice-Chairman of the Exmoor Society and an agricultural economist at Exeter University (left), and Andrew Holland of Slade Farm. (Philip Dalling)

Following the 2016 Referendum, Exmoor Society Vice-Chairman Dr Keith Howe has been reviewing the likely effect on Exmoor's farmers of life outside the EU. As an agricultural economist and senior research Fellow at Exeter University, he is professionally involved. He believes government funding for the farming industry post-Brexit will be closely linked to high environmental standards – a major plank of Exmoor Society thinking throughout the organisation's history.

Since the Referendum he has taken a broadly positive view of the future for farmers outside the EU, explaining:

> The vote inevitably meant a period of uncertainty for farmers on Exmoor and in general until a new domestic farm policy was able to replace the Common Agricultural Policy (CAP) of the EU. Unlike for many areas of the national economy, the outcome for farming is likely to prove relatively uncontroversial. There is widespread political consensus in the UK that livestock and crop production prices should be determined by free market prices. Public spending should be focused instead on paying farmers to provide a wide range of environmental products, including ecosystem services such as carbon capture, cleaner water and flood control, and the maintenance of landscape quality.

In contrast to the situation in the 1960s and for some years afterwards, there is now close co-operation and a general meeting of minds between the Society and the Exmoor National Park Authority when it comes to farming issues. In recent years too, both the Society and ENPA have worked with a new body in the form of the Exmoor Hill Farming Network, which has brought together upland farmers from across the National Park to state their determination to deliver, for people and the environment, a re-shaped agricultural policy, post-Brexit.

Echoing the views of the Exmoor Society, the Exmoor Hill Farming Network brought out a report entitled *The State of Farming on Exmoor* (2015). The Network's priorities are to keep the benefits for the public and society from upland areas such as clean water, carbon storage, diverse wildlife, sustainable recreation and tourism, and also to support viable farm businesses that maintain the special landscape features of Exmoor, whilst taking into account revised trading and support policies. The Exmoor Society in 2016 commissioned the Duchy College Rural Business School to analyse the economic state of Exmoor farms participating in their farm business survey sample. It provided evidence of the high dependence of Exmoor's farms for their viability on money received from agri-environmental schemes.

The Network and the ENPA came together, with the Exmoor Society and others, to submit to the Department for Environment, Food and Rural Affairs, a plan for post-Brexit Exmoor, under the banner of *Exmoor's Ambition*. The basis of Exmoor's ambition is the recognition of the once-in-a-generation opportunity both to protect local landscapes and to revitalise local economies.

Continuing the *Exmoor Review* tradition of spotlighting individual farmers, the journal in 2015 brought the sector firmly into the twenty-first century in an interview with Guy Thomas-Everard. The present-day representative of a family which has farmed near Dulverton for generations, Guy has become known in recent years for a willingness to embrace innovation as an aid to confronting the threats and challenges facing the industry, which for the purposes of the interview he divided into three main headings – economic, political and environmental.

He identified the main economic element facing the farmer as volatile markets, a variable beyond the power of farmers as a group, let alone as individuals, to influence. Politically, he said, the farmer is faced with the challenge of life outside the European Union and its Common Agricultural Policy, whilst environmentally speaking the industry must confront the challenges presented by climate change.

Speaking to the interviewer, former Exmoor Society trustee Richard Westcott, Guy Thomas-Everard gave an example of the way in which the three elements mentioned can overlap; a virtual doubling of the price of diesel over the space of a decade (economic and political) at a time when wetter summers (climate change) have made increased demands on tractor work.

Turning to opportunities as opposed to threats and challenges, Guy Thomas-Everard described for the *Review* the hydro-electric scheme which after just two years in operation generated 130,000 kilowatt hours and won for him the Exmoor Society's Chris Binnie Award for Sustainable Water Management, together with his successful participation in the Biomass project. An Exmoor holding farmed in many ways in a conventional sense also exports energy and reduces the impact on the environment.

Red deer stags at Cornham, Exmoor. (Nigel Stone/ENPA)

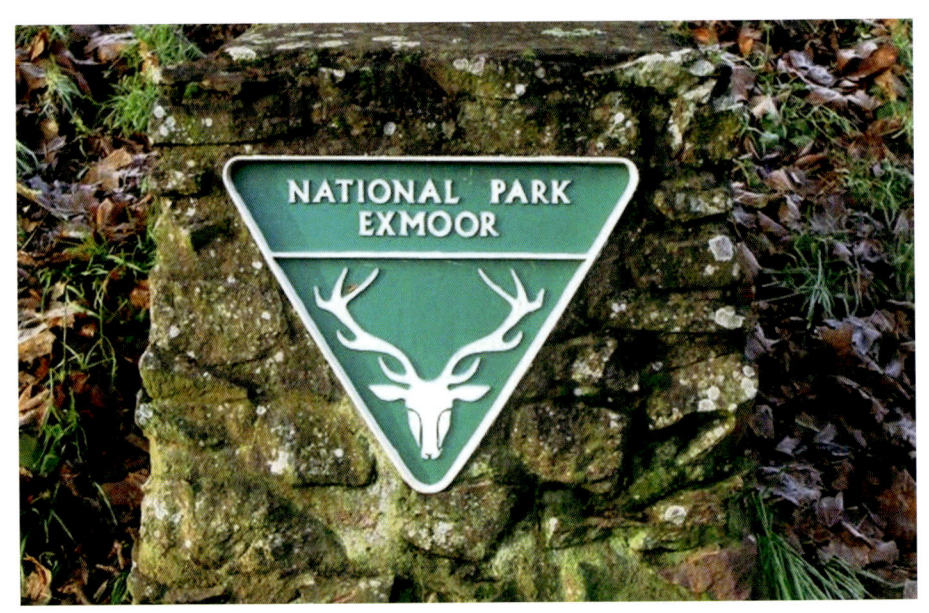

Exmoor National Park sign at Roadwater. (Philip Dalling)

Chapter Six
The Society and Country Sports

"Whatever the opinions of its individual members, the Exmoor Society as a body takes no sides about hunting."

Victor Bonham-Carter, *Exmoor Review*, 1969

Driving across Exmoor from Simonsbath to Lynton in the gathering gloom of a summer's twilight - "dimpsy" in the local dialect – my partner Brenda was the first to spot the heads of the three stags as they rose slowly above a shoulder of hillside not far from Brendon Two Gates. The stags held their position, in a perfectly symmetrical pose, the highest in the centre flanked by its fellows, for the all-too-brief time we were able to keep them in sight. It was an Exmoor moment *par excellence*.

The red deer stag, the largest wild land animal in England, standing between three and a half and four feet at the shoulder, crowned by impressive antlers, is *the* prevailing image of Exmoor. The stag's head is the official emblem of both the Exmoor Society and the Exmoor National Park Authority, and from time to time this powerful image has been borrowed "unofficially" by a variety of organisations, commercial and otherwise.

The first appearance of the emblem came in 1959, when the Exmoor National Park committees for Devon and Somerset held a public competition for a suitable motif to symbolise the Park, actually specifying that any design must include an image of a stag's head together with the words "Exmoor National Park". There were thirty-three entries, with the first prize of £50 awarded to Mr P.D. Durden of Birmingham, and the other two prize-winning designs (£10 and £5) coming from entrants from Exeter College of Art and from Backwell, Somerset.

The design was developed into cast aluminium with an enamel finish, suitable for display at entrances to the Park, with the stag's head on a green background, with white lettering. Only the majesty of a full-grown stag could challenge – and easily out-distance – the visual impact of the stag's moorland neighbour and closest rival for the status of an icon, the Exmoor pony.

Red deer have survived since prehistoric times on Exmoor, once a Royal Forest with a strict Forest Law which protected the deer in order to maintain a supply of venison and a hunting ground for the king. Today the best estimates tell of around 3,000 deer on Exmoor, living on moorland and farmland, and using the woodlands for cover.

Calves are born in June and July, usually in moorland vegetation or by the edge of woodland. A single calf is normal and twins very rare. For a few days the calf will lie quietly, well-camouflaged with dappled spots on its russet coat looking like sunlight on dead bracken. Soon it is strong enough to run with its mother and join the herd. They keep together for a year or more. Red deer eat a wide variety of food, including young shoots of heather, whortleberry, brambles, saplings and grass, acorns, fungi, berries and ivy, together with, as any Exmoor farmer will confirm, significant amounts of crops.

For all its iconic status, and the part it plays in the local economy, the red deer population has perhaps received somewhat less attention in the affairs of the Exmoor Society and in the columns of the *Review* and other publications than it might be considered to merit. Why should that be the case? The truth of the matter, of course, is that deer, together with foxes, hares, badgers and otters, have for untold generations been hunted and, despite the fact that the sport today is legal only under the strictest conditions, it remains controversial.

The subject has been a hot potato ever since the Society's creation and the organisation's policy has always been one of the strictest neutrality. But given the importance of hunting to Exmoor and the depth to which the activity is embedded within the culture of the moorland community, the Society has from time to time needed to confront the issues raised, particularly where the wellbeing of such an important component of the wildlife of the National Park is in question.

Hunting

On the subject of hunting, as with other controversial matters, the *Review* will publish opinions only when it is made clear that they express the views of the individual writer and not that of the Society. The pattern was set early on, when a comprehensive 1,800-word statement of the aims of the Society, penned by John Coleman-Cooke and the original editor, John Goodland, made no mention of the hunting question.

The first *Review* did devote some space to the chase, but only in the form of an article on the compilation of an Exmoor bibliography, that proposed listing hunt handbooks and works on the red deer of Exmoor, and hunting and riding. Subsequent editions of the journal, particularly during the 1960s, carried occasional mentions of hunting. These consisted mainly of profiles of individual huntsmen of note, a general article about the red deer in its natural habitat, of interest to naturalists, photographers and the general public as much as to the hunting fraternity, and reports of special occasions such as Boxing Day meets.

In an era when opposition to hunting with dogs was less controversial than in current times, the *Review* included quite frequent reminiscences of the hunting field, contributed by Society members who rented properties locally to allow them to pass the hunting season on the moor. In some instances these nostalgia pieces date back to the period before the First World War and are of considerable sociological value to the researcher.

Taking an Exmoor property for the stag hunting was both a sporting and a social occasion. One reminiscence involved a young woman taken to tea at Oare Manor, where the local squire maintained a sanctuary for the deer stretching all the way up Badgworthy Water to Tom's Hill. All the gates were kept locked and few people allowed in except on hunting days.

The woman's interest led to an invitation to explore the sanctuary with the squire's harbourer, who duly identified suitable stags for the next meet. The visitor took part and recalled how she had enjoyed an exhilarating run, followed by a long ride back to the rented farm and (hunting is good for the appetite) a substantial meal of bacon and eggs to round off the day. The reminiscences involved people from many different walks of life, including a husband-and-wife team of medical doctors, visiting Exmoor for the hunting just before the creation of the National Health Service, and the occasional sporting parson, including Jack Russell from Swimbridge, the original breeder of the terriers that bear his name to this day.

Although there was clearly a market in the *Review* for contributions on various aspects of hunting, and no shortage of contributors, the first report to actually concern itself with the Society's stance towards the sport did not appear until the journal had been in existence for a decade.

Victor Bonham-Carter was the author of a brief note in 1969, in the popular 'Crying the Moor' column, an entertaining miscellany of shorter items. Then editor of the *Review*, he made the Society's official position crystal clear in a brief note headed 'Hunting and Access'. He wrote: "Whatever the opinions of its individual members, the Exmoor Society as a body takes no sides about hunting."

Having made the point, he then criticised what he saw as the apathy displayed by the hunting community about one of the Society's more urgent preoccupations, the question of access to the moor. He added:"That leaves me free to say how amazed I am that hunting people seem to care so little about saving access on Exmoor. With a few notable exceptions, the great majority seem unaware even of the issues at stake – the conservation of characteristic moorland and freedom from fencing. Yet it is in their particular interest that Exmoor should remain, in essence, the open space that it still is."

The moves to ban hunting with dogs gained momentum in the years following the Second World War and these were not ignored by the Society and its officers. In his book *The Essence of Exmoor*, published in 1991, by which stage protests by hunt saboteurs were becoming increasingly common, Bonham-Carter reviewed the history of the sport in Devon and Somerset, its ups and downs, and the moves that had been made during the post-war Attlee Labour government to promote Private Members' Bills to prohibit field sports of all kinds.

A committee, chaired by John Scott Henderson KC, published a report, entitled *Cruelty to Wild Animals,* in 1951 which recognised three reasons for the existence of hunting: provision of food, sport and the control of animal population. Henderson's committee found that one suggested alternative to hunting, shooting, was just as open to inflict cruelty by wounding; that hunting was no longer the preserve of the rich, but was popular among people of moderate means, and that whilst the kill was the logical end to the chase, death was not the prime purpose.

The Henderson Committee recommended that hunting of the red deer should be allowed to continue, and in the years up to the eventual banning of hunting with dogs under the Blair administration, Henderson's findings were repeatedly endorsed by Exmoor writers and Society members as diverse as S.H. Burton, in his standard work *Exmoor*, E.R. Lloyd, author of *The Wild Red Deer of Exmoor*, and Lord Porchester, in his official report *A Study of Exmoor*.

Victor-Bonham Carter quoted Noel Allen, naturalist, author and Exmoor Society member, as believing that a major problem was the indiscriminate shooting of deer for venison, with the biggest and best deer taken with little concern for the maintenance of a balanced population. Bonham-Carter's belief was that, in reality, the conflict over hunting, of deer in particular, would never be resolved by argument, "for the subject is too emotive to be settled by reason alone". He went on to say:

> If a conclusion is ultimately reached, it will be thanks to pressure. Either the anti-hunting lobby (which is by no means the same thing as the conservation one) will ... accept hunting as a component in the campaign to protect the countryside; or hunting will be prohibited by politically and predominantly urban interests. If that happens, then it is likely that the wild red deer of Exmoor will indeed be shot and trapped to extinction.

Exmoor Society member Dick Lloyd believed that controlled culling of deer by hunting, which adhered strictly to seasonal limits, was the most humane system of selection – better, for example, than shooting. Lloyd argued:

> A deer is the property of the landowner. In the course of a single night's feeding one animal may well be the "guest" of three or more separate farmers, who are prepared to suffer limited damage to their crops on the understanding that they may enjoy their hunting, and that the Hunt authorities will do all in their power to reduce preventable harm.
> If hunting were ever to come to an end, not one in a hundred Exmoor farmers would stand for this loss. Every man's hand would be against the deer, and all the legal statutes in the book would not stop their being exterminated.

The election in 1997 of the Labour government led by Tony Blair intensified the campaign against hunting and brought closer than ever before Bonham-Carter's prediction of a legislative solution. Responsibility for the issue was handed to the Minister for Rural Affairs, Alun Michael, who set in motion a wide consultative process to which the Exmoor Society contributed.

At the heart of the Society's submission was a concern for the survival of the red deer on the moor should hunting as a means of controlling herd size be banned. Society Chairman Michael Hawkins told the Minister that the Society's conviction was that "it is simply not a valid option to do nothing except to make it illegal to hunt red deer on horseback with dogs. Such a policy would result in a rapid degrading of the red deer herd." The Society submission explained:

> On the subject of cruelty ... we make it clear that support for, or opposition to, the present practise of hunting, on moral grounds, ... is a matter for individual members. This said, we do not stand back from this important issue, as our recommendations are totally concerned with the future protection and welfare of the Exmoor Red Deer Herd ... under the present regime of control, the Exmoor herd is healthy, probably the right number, and is a visible part of the Exmoor landscape.
> Our recommendations are made with no other motive than to ensure that in the event of a ban on hunting that this situation still prevails.

The submission concluded by stating firmly that the red deer of Exmoor were "rightful inhabitants of that wild landscape" and continued: "To remove the present system of control without putting in place an equally effective form of management regime [backed by enforceable legislation] would be irresponsible and would put the herd at risk."

Graham Macro, Joint Master of the Dulverton West Foxhounds on the left and Huntsman David Nicholson (also in red) on the right. (Graham Macro)

Fly fishing on Horner Water. (Chris Guest of Exmoor Fly Fishing)

Society members who recall the atmosphere in the West Country as the Blair government drew closer to introducing legislation on hunting remember that the debate was moving towards a climax at a time when the rural community was reeling from the effects of the devastating outbreak of foot and mouth disease. Although, mercifully, this did not spread to Exmoor, the National Park (together with Dartmoor) was declared a no-go area for walkers and riders as everyone concerned attempted to stop the spread of the disease.

Michael Hawkins, writing in the Society's annual *Newsletter*, expressed the organisation's sympathy and support for farmers everywhere, saying: "We are deeply aware that their fortitude and determination to eradicate this scourge will in turn save the wildlife in the National Parks from a similar fate."

As history will record (and despite the legislation being temporarily blocked by the House of Lords) Parliament passed the Hunting Act 2004. The legislation bans the hunting of wild animals (notably foxes, deer, hares and mink) with dogs in England and Wales. The Act, which came into force on 18 February 2005, does not cover the use of dogs in the process of flushing out an unidentified wild mammal, nor does it affect drag hunting, where hounds are trained to follow an artificial scent.

Today the main Exmoor hunts – the Devon and Somerset Staghounds, the Exmoor Foxhounds, the Dulverton East Foxhounds (now re-named the Dulverton Farmers Foxhounds), Dulverton West Foxhounds, and the Minehead Harriers continue the ancient tradition of riding to hounds, attracting large fields as well as many followers. The Devon and Somerset Staghounds, which in the words of *Baily's Hunting Directory* "in theory claim to hunt the wild red deer wherever found in either county", in fact now cover the whole of the National Park, within an area bounded by the Bristol Channel on the north and west, the A361 Barnstaple to Bampton road in the south and the River Parrott in the east. Foot-following packs on Exmoor are the North Devon Beagles and the Taw Vale Beagles.

Game Shooting and Fishing

Hunting is not the only field sport to be opposed. Commercial game shooting and rough shooting by smaller syndicates and groups is also a traditional sport on Exmoor; with the commercial arm of the activity considered to be a vital part of the local economy, which provides much needed employment. Unlike in other UK National Parks there is no shooting over the moorland. Fishing, a sport with a long tradition, whether fly fishing for salmon and trout in the deep pools of many rivers within Exmoor and other National Parks, or angling for coarse species along the often murky canal banks of industrial areas, has also come under increased scrutiny in recent times.

The Exmoor Society was invited by the National Park Authority to contribute to a debate on commercial game shooting – a debate triggered by increased discussion about the developing impact of such shoots, the size and number of which has grown significantly on Exmoor over the last twenty years. Society Vice-Chairman Dr Keith Howe was asked to look into the facts and visited six shoots across the National Park and Greater Exmoor to talk to managers and gamekeepers. He reported that, in every instance, his enquiries were met with courtesy, generous expenditure of time for his benefit, and unqualified helpfulness.

Issues of concern addressed by Keith Howe included the high numbers of released birds, noise, smell, pests and contamination, litter, lead shot, the use of pharmaceuticals and the impact shoots have on landscape, public roads and rights of way. He explained:

> My own observations and published research from other bodies and individuals showed both favourable and unfavourable aspects of game shooting on Exmoor, ranging from relatively minor sources of irritation (relatively minor except to people directly affected) to those having discernible impacts more generally. As a result of my investigation the Exmoor Society made a series of ten recommendations. But ultimately, as with everything, good communication as a foundation for decision, tempered by mutual respect, is considered the best way forward.

Howe's recommendations call for recognition that the issue is a national one and that indications suggest that society as a whole does not favour game shooting. As Exmoor is nationally recognised for its exceptional qualities for the sport, what happens in the area has potential national consequences. There is also a need, he feels, for recognition that shoots organised on a small scale could be put at risk by excessive growth of the commercial sector.

He believes the economics of commercial game shooting need further exploration and more research is also required into the wider effects of the sport on other wildlife. He concluded by saying that there was evidence that Exmoor shoots take their responsibilities seriously. "Consequently, there is reason for optimism that the problems identified can be satisfactorily resolved to the benefit of all concerned."

Chapter Seven
Welcoming Visitors

"In those far-off days of 1952 ... the world – the moorland world, that is – seemed a simple place."

S. H. Burton, *Exmoor*

The advance of the plough across the acres of moorland and the Forestry Commission's vision of serried ranks of conifers marching across the unspoilt heights of the National Park were not the only nightmares to disturb the peace of some at least of the founding fathers of the Exmoor Society.

The second half of the twentieth century brought a higher standard of living and greater expectations to the working people of Great Britain. Together with higher wages and an increased feeling of job security came more leisure time and holidays with pay, all contributing to a golden era for holidays at British resorts. Car ownership among the working and lower middle classes increased rapidly, and new roads, including the first motorways, began to steadily reduce the travelling time between the highly populated urban areas in the Midlands and the North of England and the rural South West.

In addition to fighting to protect Exmoor's wild areas from development, the Society had to work out just where it stood on the thorny issue of tourism. The post-Second World War influx of holidaymakers was far greater than anything seen before, with long holiday trains from across Britain bringing thousands of visitors to the doors of Exmoor. They travelled to Minehead on what is now the privately owned West Somerset Railway and along the fringes of the moor, through Dulverton and South Molton to Barnstaple, and on to the resorts of North Devon's Gold Coast and to Ilfracombe, just a few miles from the National Park boundary near Combe Martin.

Visits to Exmoor for its exceptional scenic beauty were nothing new. Although early travel writers such as Daniel Defoe dismissed the wilder areas of Britain as little more than howling wildernesses, the Romantic poets opened eyes to the majesty of the British landscape. Over the years, Exmoor became a holiday destination, with visitors traversing its difficult terrain on horseback, by stagecoach and other horse-drawn conveyances. Towards the end of the nineteenth century, the Lynton and Barnstaple narrow-gauge railway penetrated the moor itself, whilst steamers from other Bristol Channel ports brought the new phenomenon of the day tripper to the Exmoor coast.

Bank holiday on Exmoor in the 1920s. Day visitors, including many family groups, with most people wearing their Sunday best, gather to picnic. In the foreground is the author's grandmother. (Author's collection)

Tarr Steps, one of Exmoor's honeypots. (Madeline Taylor)

The years following the First World War saw the development of motorised travel, by charabanc and later by luxury coach, which brought trippers from Barnstaple, Ilfracombe and Minehead to such apparently inaccessible beauty spots as the Heddon Valley.

When British National Parks were created from 1951 onwards, the boundaries were carefully drawn to exclude significant areas of population, particularly industrial centres and seaside resorts such as Minehead and Ilfracombe. These centres of mass tourism, with their promenades, amusement arcades and fish-and-chip restaurants, were designated as "honeypots". Such resorts provided for the kind of recreational activities that were alien to the concept of a National Park but which were likely to attract and retain outside Park boundaries the sort of visitors who, in the eyes of some people, were not particularly welcome. It was, after all, the 1950s …

Such honeypots, albeit of a more restrained nature, were also seen as part of the management of tourism *within* the National Park, intended to attract visitors in numbers to such locations as Tarr Steps, Malmsmead, Porlock and Lynton and Lynmouth, leaving the wilder areas largely free for those who preferred to spend more solitary leisure hours.

Reservations

The prospect of commercialised tourism within a National Park was not to the liking of many in the early ranks of the Society, including the influential Tim Burton, Society Chairman from 1966 to 1971, and prior to that a member of the Exmoor National Park governing body. During Burton's tenure, and for many more years, the Society was alarmed by the prospect of a veritable invasion of day trippers encouraged by the progressive opening of the M5 from the West Midlands' conurbations through Gloucestershire, Somerset and Devon, to Exeter.

In his definitive study of the National Park, *Exmoor*, Burton looked back longingly to 1952: "In those far-off days … the world – the moorland world, that is – seemed a simple place. Whatever threats existed elsewhere, Exmoor was safe. Not for us the car-borne hordes, already threatening the peace of better-known holiday areas. Most of the comparatively few visitors to heartland Exmoor came to ride, hunt, walk, fish."

> They were solitary figures in an unchanging landscape … And in those halcyon times, as memory now presents them, the walker could spend a whole summer day in solitude, entering the open moorland and leaving it where he chose. Or call at a lonely farmhouse and in exchange for his news that characteristic manifestation of Exmoor people's friendliness, a cream tea – unpriced and uncommercialised.

Don't Stray too Far from the Car, Dear!

Geoffrey Sinclair, the surveyor responsible for the highly influential Exmoor land use data, also produced some fascinating statistics relating to visitors to the National Park.

From the very early days of the National Park's existence (and doubtless long before it was designated) local people and visitors enjoyed driving onto areas like Withypool and Molland Commons and finding natural lay-bys in which to park. The older generation traditionally took out deckchairs, made tea, and relaxed. Their children (and grandchildren) paddled in streams and rivers, and played ball games. Some commentators were scornful of what they saw as a lack of ambition on the part of this type of visitor, but it was generally accepted that if they followed some simple ground rules, lit no fires and took their litter away with them when they returned home, they were harmless and part of the rich variety of Exmoor life.

Horse riders on Exmoor. (Nigel Stone/ENPA)

Sinclair observed their numbers and their habits through in-depth surveys on Withypool Common. He noted that the tourist season there was concentrated around the months of June to September, but extended earlier and later at weekends. The visitors he monitored came almost entirely by car, with the relatively few horse riders to be seen being local. Eighty per cent of the sample he observed in August 1967 were day visitors to Exmoor from other parts of the South West.

The surveys made on Withypool Common were taken at midday, and were designed to cover three different types of weather conditions. A striking feature discovered by Sinclair and his team was that Sunday visitors tended to stay firmly within 100 yards of their vehicles. He also discovered that horse riders were loathe to use the Common on Sundays because of the large numbers of people and cars clustered around the entrances. In any case, most equestrians, unlike the motorists, lived near enough to be able to visit the Common on weekdays.

On Sundays the cars contained family groups averaging 4.6 people and the average length of stay per group was three hours, as opposed to twenty minutes which was the weekday average. No coach parties were seen, owing to the nature of the roads leading to the Common, but several large vans helped swell the visitor figures.

Chapter Seven: Welcoming Visitors

From any perspective, and when considered in the context of the declared aim of the National Park movement to open up the countryside to the wider public, it seems a strange attitude for a declared socialist like Burton to adopt.

It was certainly not the approach adopted by the Exmoor Society as a whole. In fact, in the very early days, the *Exmoor Review* had called for a balanced response to the whole issue of tourism. In the fourth volume of the annual publication there had appeared an unsigned note as part of the Society's annual report to its members for the period 1961-62. The Society was still being steered by its founder and first Chairman, John Coleman-Cooke, and it is likely that the words that follow, although published anonymously, came from his fluent pen under the simple heading 'Tourists':

> To many members of the Society, "tourists" are anathema. We object to them if they clog the roads, we object even more if they forsake the roads and invade our cherished haunts. To farmers they are a mixed blessing; welcome, perhaps to the farmer's wife, unwelcome if they do not observe the Country Code. Ironically for us, the farmers seldom discriminate between a tourist and a preservationist!

> We must not be selfish; we enjoy Exmoor through the year without contributing much to it. Through our Museum [recently opened at Lynton] and the *Review* we hope we will enhance the enjoyment of the moor for many tourists, and through our other works we hope to preserve the Moor as an open space, as well as a tourist attraction. We welcome those tourists who respect the fact that many people earn their living here, and that many others come to get away from the madding crowd.

From time to time over the last six decades the *Exmoor Review* has carried some fascinating accounts of holidaymaking on Exmoor. In most instances, the experiences related conform to the image of the ideal Exmoor holidaymaker propagated by Burton.

There are accounts of holidays, between and following the world wars, spent riding for pleasure across the moor and, at a different pace, following the Devon and Somerset Staghounds, staying in farmhouse accommodation with host families who as the years passed would become firm friends, and helping with chores such as rounding up the livestock. One of the first Christmastide articles the author wrote for his long-running *Devon Life* column 'Man on the Moor' told a rather sad tale of such an instance.

The children of the hill-farming Reed family had helped their mother to bake a Christmas cake, mince pies and other seasonal treats. When a party of regular visitors arrived unexpectedly just days before Christmas, they were

For Exmoor hill farmers in the early 1920s income from tourism was just as important as today. The young Nettie Reed (pictured at her home at Knighton Farm) recalled how regular holiday visitors arrived unexpectedly close to Christmas and ate all the seasonal goodies the family was saving for the big day.
(Nettie Reed)

not at first disturbed. But the only fare their mother could muster, feeling the need to display traditional Exmoor hospitality, was the family's own seasonal goodies. The visitors ate the lot and, with cash scarce, there was no hope of replacing the cake and mince pies!

It was a mode of tourism far removed from the day trippers arriving by steamer in Lynmouth Bay, a fact emphasised by the revelation that many of the families who visited the moor annually brought their own maids to help in the farmhouse, and their own grooms for their horses.

Also typical of the type of tourists who doubtless won the approval of Burton and many of his peers were the Oxford Inklings, the group of literary personalities – C.S. Lewis, J.R.R. Tolkien, Charles Williams and their friends – who wanted nothing more than good walking country, a clean and comfortable bed, simple, plain food, and a pint or two of honest ale in an unspoilt village tavern.

Jack Lewis, best known to a modern audience as the creator of *The Chronicles of Narnia*, spent more than one Exmoor holiday of that description with his brother Warren and friends. Lewis' first visit to the area in 1920 was, out of keeping with his later image as a Christian apologist, a clandestine affair. He was just twenty-one, still at university and financially dependent upon his father, a Northern Ireland solicitor. He told his father that he would be exploring the moor with a male friend, but in fact his companion was Janie Moore, the 45-year-old mother of an Army friend, killed in the First World War, and her daughter Maureen.

Lewis and the Moores returned in 1925, travelling by charabanc from the railway station at Minehead to County Gate, for a stay at Malmsmead. He liked modern tourism no more than Burton, writing: "It was the first time either of us had travelled in this way. We didn't like it, either for comfort or safety." Malmsmead was much more to his liking and he recorded in his diary:

"The whole thing realised my best dreams. The farm house stands under a wood of fir, with one field between it and the river. The rooms were comfortable and the supper good."

In 1931 Lewis and three friends embarked upon an Exmoor walking tour. They visited Luccombe, climbed to Dunkery Beacon, visited the Valley of Rocks and explored the fringes of The Chains at Challacombe. A thick fog, anathema to the average tourist, delighted Lewis, who described it as "revealing the moor at its grimmest".

From the 1960s onwards (he died in 2006), Tim Burton increasingly distrusted the claims of the importance tourism represented to the Exmoor economy. He wrote:

> Tourism is, we are often told, vital to the economic life of the inhabitants of the Exmoor National Park. (How vital is vital?) There is an element of truth in the claim, of course, but the tourist industry, through its well-organised and well-funded organisations, blatantly overstates its case.
>
> Second only to the National Farmers Union, the tourism lobby manages to exert an influence on national and local policymakers that is wholly disproportionate to the number of people that it represents. Nobody has ever succeeded in quantifying the benefits that tourism brings. Some of them are recognisable and only a fool would ignore them; for instance shops, pubs, cafes open all-the-year-round would not survive but for the profits of "the season". But we need to look with a much more sceptical eye at tourism's larger claims and its insatiable demands for more public money to be spent on advertising, providing tourist facilities (unused for nine months of the year) and subsidising hotel and property improvements that should be paid for out of private profits.

The National Park movement as a whole, and Malcolm MacEwen in particular, could be openly hostile towards tourism. MacEwen accused Park authorities of being "preoccupied with promoting particular areas less for their real qualities than for commercial gimmicks such as *Lorna Doone* on Exmoor". MacEwen disliked what he termed "the degradation of natural beauty by the superficial attractions of souvenir shops, ice cream vans and other devices for parting visitors from their money".

Spreading the Benefits

It was not all criticism. The plea in the 1962 edition of the *Review* for a tolerant view of tourism was echoed by a subsequent Chairman of the Society, Michael Hawkins, who held the post for eight years from 1995 to 2003. Hawkins never forgot that his first introduction to the scenic delights of Exmoor had come from the front seat of a motor coach. It has to be

Backpackers in the 1970s. (Exmoor Society Archive)

When car ownership was still relatively restricted, touring coaches were an important factor in Exmoor tourism. A once familiar Royal Blue coach and the still common National Express ease their way along Church Street, Dunster, in 1974. (Exmoor Society Archive)

said immediately that he had something of a vested interest, as the coach in question was owned by his family and was driven on many excursions by his father. Michael Hawkins also spent his own working life associated with transport, serving for seventeen years as County Engineer and Planning Officer for the County of Devon. In the *Exmoor Review* of 1996, he explained that among other things his time was spent "in controlling and coping with the relentless growth of traffic, including the co-ordination of public transport, which included the curtailing of the intrusion of coaches into the county's two national parks!"

> Despite all of this I still recall with affection the thrill that I experienced as a small boy sitting next to my father on those sumptuous, gleaming Scarlet coaches, with the luxurious smell of leather and the highest quality upholstery, as we climbed slowly out of the lower plain through the wooded valleys onto the open moorland and then being able to roam free until it was time to move on to the next exciting stopping place and finally, with any luck, to Horner Woods for tea! ... The tour did not simply take passengers to a destination; the trip was made more interesting by frequent stops for the driver to explain points of interest.

Tourism's Contribution

The leading figures in the Exmoor Society who worried about the impact increased tourism would have on the landscape and culture of the moor mostly lived long enough to accept that many of the worst fears of an unsustainable number of visitors flooding down the M5 motorway were, happily, unfounded.

In fact the most up-to-date figures for visits to Exmoor in the twenty-first century reveal that only 18 per cent of visitors are from heavily populated regions of the West and East Midlands and the North of England. Precise figures do not survive for tourism on Exmoor in the immediate post-war golden era of holidays in Britain (staycations as the modern term has it) and more people probably visited the National Park from the North and Midlands in the days of the packed holiday trains to Minehead and Ilfracombe than they do today.

The package holidays of the 1960s, cruises and the increasingly exotic destinations opened up by air travel for all, have also played a part in keeping tourism on Exmoor at a sustainable level. Half of all visitors now come from within the South West region (including the majority of day visitors), and approximately two-thirds from southern England. The proportional spread of domestic visitors has remained relatively consistent over the years. The scenic beauty and peace and quiet of the countryside also have a major influence on the age profile of visitors, which is skewed towards the older generations. Those aged forty-five plus now account for 70 per cent of all visitors to Exmoor and the trend is increasing, with the comparative figure in 2005 being much lower, at 59 per cent.

Currently, Exmoor welcomes more than two million visitors annually. In terms of what brings them to the area, little has changed since the creation of the National Park – the moor's wide-ranging special qualities of natural beauty, wildlife, cultural heritage and the varied recreational opportunities afforded to visitors. It is estimated that tourism on Exmoor brings in over £105m to the economy and creates the equivalent of over 2,000 full-time jobs (around 20 per cent of the entire population of less than 11,000 people!).

The National Park Authority and the Visit Exmoor organisation, with the support of the Society, are keen to achieve a better balance where age profile is concerned and attract more young people to the Park. The Exmoor Society today is largely supportive of the policies of the National Park Authority in the area of tourism, particularly in such initiatives as the annual Dark Skies Festival and efforts to encourage interest in flora and fauna, especially amongst young people. The ENPA's desire for greater inclusivity, encouraging more members of ethnic groups to discover and enjoy the National Park, is also supported.

Hawkins commented that for those who saw the motor car as the foremost threat to the peace and tranquility of Exmoor:

> The mere mention of coaches ever being allowed to penetrate into the National Park is enough to bring about apoplexy. Yet for a period of nearly half a century between the end of the First World War and the mid-1960s the charabanc, and later the luxury coach, in surprisingly large numbers, traversed Exmoor on a daily basis during the holiday season to all the well-known locations. When the First War ended, the survivors – suddenly released from its horrors – were determined to exercise their new-found freedom and so the great British holiday became an established part of working class life … the bus and charabanc, which had become reliable forms of transport, provided the only means by which most people could ever hope to enjoy the pleasures of travel.

Michael Hawkins' attitude demonstrated, if nothing else, the breadth of views that existed within the Exmoor Society.

On the subject of tourism, as with most of the major issues which have challenged the society over its six decades, tact and diplomacy have played a major role in the solution of disputes and disagreements.

Towards Sustainable Tourism

Society officers have frequently and fruitfully listened to the views of various parties whose interests might have been dismissed as being at odds with the organisation's most cherished beliefs. The ideas expressed by these people might not always have become part of Society policy, but have nevertheless contributed to discussions over the future of Exmoor. An interesting and well-reasoned contribution to the tourism debate came in the last years of the twentieth century from an Exmoor hotelier. It was notable for suggesting a partnership approach to tourism, something the Exmoor Society had espoused during the debates on land reclamation and which, eventually, had largely triumphed.

Donald Wade, who wrote a substantial article for the 1998 edition of the *Exmoor Review*, owned the Anchor Hotel at Porlock Weir and the associated Ship Inn at the same venue. His views suggest that those visitors who patronised his own establishments were very different from the hordes of trippers feared by Burton and others in the days when the M5 motorway was being planned.

Wade argued that he was convinced that the main reason guests stayed at his hotel was to enjoy the beauty of Exmoor:

Carry on Sir Billy!

When the Butlin's Holiday Camp at Minehead was first proposed in 1961, the Exmoor Society was asked by the Council for the Preservation of Rural England for its views on the development. The Society decided not to lodge an objection, arguing that the site earmarked for the camp lay just outside the National Park boundary, and accepting that the provision of facilities for holidaymakers was one of the fundamental tenets of the National Parks and Access to the Countryside Act 1949.

A holiday camp outside the Park boundary fitted in to the "honeypot" theory of concentrating mass tourism, with the hope of preventing overcrowding of the wilder areas. It was also believed that the camp would not seriously spoil the view from within the National Park, although the later development of the large marquee-like structures did not fit so well with the Society's values.

This was not the Society's only contact with Sir Billy Butlin's organisation. As the 1970s began, there was much discussion on the implications for the countryside of the greater amount of leisure time considered to be on the horizon. The subject was tackled in a thoughtful 1971 *Review* article by Paul Winterforde-Young, who had worked for Boys' Clubs in London and Birmingham and for the Duke of Edinburgh's Award Scheme in Devon.

His article, 'Your Leisure and Mine', began from the premise that the "less work, more leisure" forecast as the norm in the 1970s "may mean a lot of trouble unless we prepare for it. Free time can easily be abused, and boredom is the greatest single obstacle to happiness for people of any age ... Preparation and thought are needed – not to organise leisure but to organise for leisure, a very different thing, and most necessary in this overcrowded island of ours." Winterforde-Young believed the Exmoor Society, often in partnership with other organisations, had a significant role to play in educating the public.

An example he cited was the survey into the possibility of converting part of the abandoned Taunton-Barnstaple railway line into a leisure route. This received the backing of the Exmoor Society and Butlin's – one a voluntary group, one commercial – both of whom realised that "Exmoor is far too precious a place to be allowed to drift into chaotic development, or conversely to remain static in the face of all the pressure that is building up against it ... If Exmoor is to retain its character in the years ahead as a harbour of wildlife and a region of moorland, forest and farmland, of great landscape beauty, providing reasonable access for you and me, then we have got to accept the idea of 'organisation for leisure.'"

I also know from their conversations that they are all concerned to ensure that Exmoor retains and enhances its beauty. It seems from this that, perhaps without even knowing it, guests at our hotel, and probably the majority of visitors to Exmoor, have a personal commitment to sustainable tourism. The essence of the concept known as "sustainable tourism" is to ensure that decisions and actions taken today involving tourism on Exmoor have, as far as possible, no adverse effect on the Exmoor of tomorrow – no adverse effect on future visitors' enjoyment of its beauty, its landscape and seascape, its wildlife and its cultural heritage.

Wade did not deny that conflicts of interest, such as a planning proposal which involved a "limited" adverse effect on the environment, would arise on occasions between business and the conservation lobby as represented by the Exmoor Society and other bodies. He nevertheless added: "Although at first sight this might seem a mixture of terms, many tourist operators on Exmoor probably view themselves as custodians. This is both ethically sound and good, enlightened self-interest. The majority of visitors come (and return) because of the beauty of the area, if their enjoyment was reduced, so would the chances of a return trip."

The hotelier mentioned several initiatives launched at his business concerns designed to actively encourage visitors to help with the task of conserving Exmoor. Both the Anchor Hotel and the Ship Inn encouraged visitors to make a modest financial contribution (matched by the management) to local projects. These had taken the form of helping to fund the re-planting of broadleaf trees along a coastal walk, some research on Exmoor's dormice, and footpath maintenance.

Bonham-Carter's Pragmatism
In contrast to the surprisingly harsh verdict on tourism espoused by Tim Burton and Malcolm MacEwen, Victor Bonham-Carter went to considerable lengths in his writings (at roughly the same period when Burton and MacEwan made their major pronouncements on the issue) to acknowledge that different groups of holidaymakers had vastly differing desires. He reserved much of his scepticism at this period for the National Park Authority and its declared intention of "absorbing people without intrusion in the landscape".

The ENPA in the closing decade of the twentieth century, said Bonham-Carter, drew comfort, mistakenly in his view, from statistics which seemed to suggest that the number of visitors to Exmoor overall had changed little in the past twenty years, despite the construction of the M5 Motorway and the North Devon Link Road, "plus the proliferation of brown enamel notices on these and other highways directing motorists towards the National Park".

His attitude towards visitors who arrived by car, coach or motorcycle was characteristically more tolerant and pragmatic than that of some of his contemporaries within the Exmoor Society. He wrote:

> Exmoor is small and accessible and easy to enjoy without having to stay overnight. Nearly everybody comes by [motor transport], even if they intend to walk or ride a horse. The majority are car-bound. They drive around the beauty spots, pull off the road along stretches of moorland, take out chairs and rugs, picnic, admire the view, go for short walks and let the children romp in the heather. *That is as it should be and fulfils one of the objects of the National Park.* [Italics added]

Bonham-Carter in general terms approved of the substantial amount of car parking provided by the National Park Authority and private providers but nevertheless warned: "Saturation is only a matter of time. The unpalatable fact is that the provision of parking, allied to the policy of attracting visitors to a handful of 'honeypot' [locations] ... is at best a holding operation."

Turning aside from the fears of saturation by the motor car to the question of tourist economics, in *The Essence of Exmoor* Victor Bonham-Carter's assessment of the situation accepted what contemporary calculations appeared to show – that, already, tourism employed more people and generated more income on Exmoor than farming and forestry, usually seen as the primary sources of work within the National Park. He concluded:

> That would seem to justify its expansion on economic grounds alone, so long as it stays within bounds and does not turn into Frankenstein's monster. The ENPA believes it can cope with the problem ... by enlarging the scope of its Information Centres, by continuing to organise guided walks and talks, by expanding the work of the Ranger service, by encouraging the visits of school groups and by co-operating with other interested organisations ... The question is – can it be sustained and will it succeed?

Bonham-Carter had misgivings about the development of Information Centres by the Park Authority at popular spots including Dulverton, Dunster and Lynmouth. Accepting that tourism was important to the economy of the area, he nevertheless believed that it was the role of the Authority to guide rather than to initiate enterprise and in all matters ensure that development was compatible with conservation. The Information Centres, in his view:

> ... conduct brisk and profitable business in the sale of merchandise and ... publications ... about Exmoor, [veer] very closely to promotion as opposed to interpretation. The point is emphasised by ... *The Exmoor Visitor*, the free National Park newspaper ... [that] contains a mixture of

Holiday makers at Watermouth Bay.
(James Walker, ENPA)

articles, a programme of guided walks and pages of advertisements about accommodation, places to visit, and a mass of other commercial information. The inference is obvious. The more publicity, the greater the problems in containing the invasion that has already all but overwhelmed some of the other National Parks, where overcrowding and erosion have become twin nightmares. Appetite grows with eating. It is a classic dilemma.

In view of Bonham-Carter's doubts about the propriety of the National Park Information Centres adopting a commercial role in addition to acting purely as a dispenser of information and guidance, it is somewhat ironic that the Exmoor Society today is, in a suitably restrained way, a part of the National Park's tourist industry. Its new Resource Centre in Dulverton, opened in 2015, includes a modest but attractively laid out shop, selling books, notelets, limited edition prints, calendars, and Christmas cards. The Society's own imprint, *Exmoor Studies*, a series of booklets covering subjects from the iconic Exmoor pony to biographies of the many writers who have chronicled the area over the years, allows visitors to study chosen aspects of the National Park in some depth. More substantial works by the many authors of repute who have covered every aspect of Exmoor life can also be browsed, whilst other items simply provide a reasonably priced souvenir to be taken home as a reminder of a special place.

The clause in the 1949 Act which created National Parks in Great Britain, stipulating that the interests of agriculture and forestry must be taken into account during the Park administration's decision making processes, was seen as favouring the landowning interest. Similarly, a second clause in the Act, which declared that a major intent behind the concept of National Parks was the opening up of the nation's finest and wildest landscapes to the wider public, appeared to many to provide justification for opening the floodgates to mass tourism – a force they saw as potentially as destructive as land reclamation and conifer planting.

Public Access

Some of the issues surrounding tourism and access took decades to resolve. A prime example was the thorny question of public access to the Commons, an issue which was the subject of considerable concern to the Exmoor Society from its very early days but was not finally resolved until the start of the twenty-first century.

These often extensive tracts of Exmoor (and other National Parks) not only possessed great natural beauty but also constituted an important resource for raising livestock. In 1958, the year of the Society's birth, the Commons had been described as the nation's "last uncommitted reserves of land". The Commoners who enjoyed the much coveted right to graze their stock on the Commons were apprehensive about the effect on the land of significant tourist use.

The Exmoor Society first debated the issue in the mid-1960s when a trip to one of the National Park's many areas of common land, at locations such as Withypool, Molland, and Brendon, was a growing attraction not just for visitors but for locals too. At the time the Society concluded that multipurpose use of the Commons was desirable and need not lead to conflict between the graziers and the visitors.

The public had no legal right of access to most of the Commons; access here was only by custom, a situation, the Society contended, that was not good enough. The Society *Newsletter* for 1982 dealt with the subject at some length, making the point that the precise nature of access by custom had never been defined and could consequently be withdrawn at any time. The only solution, said the Society, was to make it a public right, subject to safeguards to ensure responsible behaviour on the part of the public and so protect the interests of the Commoners.

The Society backed the national campaign for legal access rights but also urged the National Park Authority to enter into local agreements with the landowners and those who held Commoners grazing rights and lay down guidelines for recreation on foot and on horseback. In exchange the Authority should make available funds for land management, greatly enhancing the situation for owners and visitors alike.

The Society *Newsletter* ventured the opinion that a solution to the issue "would require legislation and will take time", adding that "politicians of all parties have been reluctant to grasp this particular nettle". The forecast of a long-drawn-out campaign for legal right of public access proved accurate; it was not until the year 2000 that the right was conceded in the Blair government's Countryside and Rights of Way Act which passed into law that year.

Today Exmoor's largest Common, Brendon, is administered by a Statutory Commons Council, representing the landowners and the members of what was formerly known as the Brendon Commoners Association. Brendon Common had enjoyed a substantial measure of public access right since the 1930s.

When the rules and procedures for the Commons Council were formulated it was accepted that Brendon Common was one of Exmoor's "tourism honeypot" destinations, with the Simonsbath to Lynton road which bisects the Common affording some of the best vistas of open moorland in the whole of the National Park, together with fine views of the Exmoor coastline, the Bristol Channel and South Wales.

From the standpoint of 2020, whilst visits to Exmoor continue to rise in popularity, the worst fears of Society members and landowners and farmers of the National Park being flooded with a tidal wave of day trippers in search of candy floss and fish and chips at every turn have, happily, proved to be largely groundless. The last thing the steelworkers and coal miners of South Yorkshire and the mill hands from Greater Manchester who in the 1930s battled for the right to roam the moors of the Peak District wanted was the encouragement of the grosser aspects of commercial tourism.

Today's public in general is more sophisticated and environmentally aware than their counterparts in earlier times and has generally responded responsibly to the significant degree of access now available. The point was conceded as far back as 1986 by Guy Somerset, the then Chairman of the Exmoor Society. Somerset accepted that Exmoor had not suffered as badly as some other National Parks from sheer weight of numbers, although the volume of cars and presence at times of too many people was an issue in the wilder areas of the Park.

He called for "a balanced and positive policy to deal with a delicate problem", acknowledging that a large number of local traders, farmers, and others depended in whole or part, on visitors. Somerset nonetheless emphasised that the first priority of the Exmoor Park Authority must be to preserve and enhance the natural beauty of the countryside, alongside the statutory duty to promote the enjoyment of the Park by the public. Striking a note of optimism, he concluded : "Those who come to the Park are the last to want to see it ruined by over-exploitation."

A Rail Conversion Vision that Ran into the Buffers

Disused railway lines are a favourite resort for walkers and cyclists throughout Britain. With unobtrusive resurfacing, access points, car parking and refreshment facilities at former stations, impressive viaducts and mysterious tunnels to traverse and the occasional restored signal box and other relics of past glories to discover, railway trails make an interesting expedition for all age groups.

In 1969 the Exmoor Society invested much time and effort in attempting to promote what, had it proved successful, would have been one of the earliest and longest railway trails in Great Britain. The former Great Western Railway's line from Taunton to Barnstaple, which ran along the fringes of Exmoor, via Wiveliscombe, Dulverton and South Molton, closed in the autumn of 1966. The section beyond East Anstey was quickly sold into private ownership and much of the track bed later disappeared under the North Devon Link Road.

The twenty-two mile stretch between East Anstey, in North Devon, and Norton Fitzwarren in Somerset remained in the ownership of British Rail, who agreed to the Society's request that the section should not be sold until the possibility of its conversion for recreational use had been fully explored. The Society commissioned a feasibility study from Ross Gray and Michael Dower of the Dartington Amenity Research Trust that also included the Taunton to Minehead railway line whose closure was announced in 1970.

The study, which can be viewed in the Society's Resource Centre at Dulverton, was very thorough. However, the working party established by Somerset County Council to examine the matter eventually reached the conclusion that the Greenway scheme as a whole was not financially realistic. Nor was the conversion of the section from Dulverton station (situated some two miles from the town, at Brushford) to East Anstey, a distance of four miles, worth pursuing. The Exmoor Society's vision of the Greenway was well in advance of thinking across the National Park movement, although today there are a great many well-used trails utilising former railway lines.

Visitors to Exmoor can, however, visit selected locations on the former West Somerset Mineral Railway, which ran from Watchet Harbour via an impressive rope-worked incline powered by a winding house still visible today, to iron-ore mines on the Brendon Hills. Michael Hawkins, then Society Chairman, played a leading role in encouraging the preservation of the remains of the Mineral Railway, chairing a working group, today's West Somerset Mineral Railway Association, to drive forward the preservation project. North Devon has trails along the former railway lines radiating from Barnstaple to Torrington and Ilfracombe.

PART THREE:
The Present Day and into the Future

Chapter Eight
Broadening the Society's Role

"A great burden of work will fall on us, but also great credit if the work is done well. This will be something tangible and will help our transition from being a small band of idealists to being a body with responsibilities and care."

John Goodland, *Exmoor Review*, 1961

The small group of campaigners who came together in the autumn of 1958 to form the Society could have been forgiven for concentrating their limited resources solely on the burning question of land use and becoming, effectively, a single-issue pressure group. The temptation to direct all available funding and human resources towards conservation must have been substantial. The threat facing the moor was very real and a primary obstacle the Society had to overcome to achieve its aims was the vested interest of powerful bodies and individuals, both in the area of national and local government, and of private landed interests.

Had the Society's early campaigning proved fruitless, there was a very real possibility that in the not-too-distant future there would be no National Park worthy of the name; no exceptional landscape to, as the organisation proudly proclaims on its website in 2020, "protect and promote for the benefit of all". To their everlasting credit, the founders of the Society determined to take a broad-brush approach and create an organisation that was much more than a simple pressure group. In the early days it was often accused of tiresome meddling and of interference in affairs of which it had no real understanding – its members labeled "outsiders".

The Society soon dispelled the charge that it lacked specialist knowledge by enlisting the help of people expert in their own fields of activity. And any force the jibe of "outsiders" may have carried was quickly dissipated by the recruitment to the Society ranks of people with an immaculate Exmoor pedigree, or a deep commitment to the area where they had chosen to take up residence and immerse themselves in the life of the National Park.

Exmoor Review, *2020*. (Exmoor Society)

Whatever the pressures exerted by the battles to halt the ploughing of moorland and the planting of conifers, the Society from the beginning devoted much time and effort to celebrating the social and cultural life of Exmoor, an aspect of the National Park as full of tradition as the age-old landscapes and traditional methods of husbandry and cultivation which had prompted the creation of the organisation.

The *Exmoor Review*

Over the six decades and more since the battle for The Chains brought the Exmoor Society into being, the glue which has held the organisation together and propagated its message far and wide has been the *Exmoor Review*.

The *Review* very soon became a major weapon in the Society's armoury, with expert analyses of the problems facing the Park identified and discussed in its columns under the names of people distinguished in their fields. Important as its role as a watchdog and as a vehicle for co-ordinating campaigns and suggesting solutions was to prove – a role just as vital and relevant in 2020 as in 1959 – the *Review* from its very first edition was much more than a medium for keeping the Society's widely scattered membership up to date with major issues.

The publication was the vehicle for recording and promoting the Society's activities. It quickly developed into a high-quality countryside journal full of diverse and well-written material, celebrating the landscape and its communities and, returning again to the words of the modern-day mission statement proclaimed by the website, working "to help everyone appreciate the wonder the Park can offer, and organise activities that encourage visitors and locals alike to enjoy it in as many ways as possible".

The *Review* was, and remains, an annual publication and it was soon realised that newsletters and other means of communication, which today include press releases, a website and other social media, were necessary to keep members in touch with events as they occurred. What the *Review* did extremely well from its beginnings was to publish serious commentary on major issues, contributed by quality writers with the sort of expertise in their chosen subjects that could not be dismissed by the cynics, and to look ahead to how the Society intended to pursue its aims.

The campaigns to save Exmoor's moorland from the plough and from the threat of intensive afforestation dragged on with such little success that the group's doughtiest campaigners came at times near to despair. Nevertheless, the Society did achieve a great deal in the cultural context, with projects that were not only desirable in their own right but also broadened the organisation's appeal and helped to attract a wide variety of new members and supporters.

In the columns of the *Review*, blending in well with the serious, campaigning material, was a wealth of coverage of the abundant history, traditions, myths and legends of the moor. The journal has throughout the decades maintained its high standards and is at the same time both intensely informative and immensely entertaining. It celebrates all that is unique about Exmoor, its flora and fauna, its heaths and grass moors, spectacular coastline, woodlands, streams and rivers, wide (and dark) skies, peace, tranquility and wildness. All of these aspects are brought to the reader via poetry, prose and high-class photography.

The first issue of the *Review* appeared in the autumn of 1959, printed by Cox, Printers, Williton and, from the start, aimed to attract a wider audience than simply the paid-up members, who received a free copy. A feature of the first edition (and of several subsequent numbers) was the inclusion of a full list of members and the cities, towns and villages where they lived. In autumn 1959 this membership totalled just under 200 people. As the membership grew, eventually to a figure of several thousands, it became impossible to find the space to continue this listing. The *Review* was on sale widely across the moorland villages, often delivered by local agents, and at first cost one shilling and sixpence.

As the second decade of the twenty-first century draws to a close, the Society has an impressive array of competitions and award schemes. The very first edition of the *Review* included details of these and initiatives designed to encourage active involvement among both residents of the National Park and visitors. The first entries in a youth essay competition, designed to encourage an appreciation of Exmoor and the ability to write good English, produced a well-balanced response.

The winning essays, reprinted in the 1960 edition of the *Review*, covered many aspects of life on Exmoor. They included a short item on sport on the moor, with the emphasis on shooting rabbits, amusingly written in West Country dialect by a fourteen-year-old boy, John Bowden. This had originally appeared in the Christmas edition of the Combe Martin Secondary School magazine. A longer piece, by thirteen-year-old William French, discussed beekeeping, whilst Alan Johnson, also thirteen, saluted the memory of the Exmoor Home Guard (of which his father was a member) during the Second World War.

The Society supports tourism at sustainable levels, local employment and business, and works to support thriving villages with housing, schools and services that attract and encourage visitors, co-operating and connecting with other organisations, and lobbying locally and nationally, working in partnership to achieve its aims. The foresight of the early officers and members steered the Society away from the dangers of too narrow a focus. The way in which their original aims and beliefs have been steadily developed over more than six decades, and the fact that the Society in 2020 is not only thriving but has retained all of its relevance, is a tribute to their vision.

Walking the Moor
A primary form of sustainable tourism is walking and since the start of the current century the Society has been a major provider of guided walks on Exmoor, covering the pre-eminent areas of landscape, wildlife and the cultural heritage of the area included within the boundaries of the National Park.

Each year the publication of the new season's programme is an eagerly awaited event. That for 2020 was released early in the New Year and featured twenty-two walks, of different lengths and covering a wide variety of themes. The walks start from a number of accessible locations across the moor, and provide opportunities to discover prehistoric sites, follow in the footsteps of figures from literature and the arts associated with Exmoor and view the

Walking on North Hill, near Bossington. (Jennifer Rowlandson)

moorland landscapes that inspired them. The fascinating history of Exmoor's settlements, once explained by a knowledgeable walk leader, will enhance future visits to village and hamlet, whilst other walks focus on plants and wildlife – although with no guarantee of sightings!

The leaders are volunteers who enjoy sharing their time, knowledge and passion for Exmoor. Members and non-members alike are welcome to join the walks, which are free, although donations towards administrative costs are very much appreciated.

Exmoor at a Crossroads

A major contribution to conserving and enhancing the natural splendour of the moor and its associated flora and fauna came together in the Exmoor Moorland Landscape Project, which ran from 2010 to 2015, supported financially by The Heritage Lottery Fund, the Exmoor National Park Authority and others.

The Society's *Moorlands at a Crossroads* report, published in 2004, was the base document on which the scheme was developed. The project championed the National Park's moorland landscape over the five-year period and involved a range of people from all walks of life – farmers, tourists, local business people, ecologists, students and the retired. Projects undertaken included landscape improvements, of both a major and a minor nature, the provision of apprenticeships and moor-keepers, moorland classroom activities and archaeological digs.

Given the overall title of 'The Heart of Exmoor', the scheme was a partnership of twelve organisations chaired by Arabella Amory, an Exmoor Society trustee, and driven by project staff. At the end of the five-year period the organisations involved undertook to embed the legacy of the project within their day-to-day policies and activities.

Planning Issues

During the opening years of the new century the Society was active in the areas where issues stemming from national policies, particularly in the field of planning, took on a strongly localised form. All planning applications submitted to the responsible body, the Exmoor National Park Authority, were made available to the Society and carefully scrutinised before a decision was taken as to whether or not to express an opinion.

Encouraging changes in the operation of the planning system were detected by the Society's landscape advisory group. An appeal to retain an unauthorised communications mast at Beacon Down was rejected by the Inspector, for reasons based on landscape criteria. A decision by the Society's executive committee to object to the proposal for a large-scale wind farm outside the Park's boundaries on the grounds that it affected the setting of the Park, its landscape character and the quality of its special features was endorsed by the National Park Authority, which agreed to register an objection. At this time the Society was also active in encouraging policy campaigns on issues such as reducing clutter in the landscape, starting with overhead wires.

A planning issue with landscape implications hit the media headlines in 2008, which because of the location involved could be described as a second battle for The Chains. What at first sight appeared to be simply a routine agenda item for a meeting of the ENPA developed into a furore, dominating local (and occasionally national) media headlines for nearly six months. It spawned a grassroots protest movement calling itself the Exmoor Revolting Peasants Party, generated calls from the local Member of Parliament for resignations from the Park Authority, and involved the Exmoor Society in a financial controversy.

The issue revolved around the question of what should be done with Blackpitts Bungalow, a former shepherd's dwelling, somewhat on the fringes of The Chains, next to the Simonsbath to Lynton Road and situated some twenty miles away from that ruling criterion of modern life, a supermarket. The bungalow, which had been empty for two years before the controversy erupted, with its surrounding land, was purchased by the National Park Authority for £238,900.

The ENPA's intention was to demolish the bungalow and its outbuildings, which included the remains of a barn thought to be more than 200 years old, and restore the site to a natural state, a process referred to as "re-wilding". The Authority justified its proposal by saying that the house and plot, had it been sold to a private buyer, could have been re-developed in a way inappropriate to its location.

The Exmoor Society backed the ENPA, describing its plan as "a brave decision" and promised to provide a sum of up to £100,000 from two charities to facilitate the clearance and "re-wilding" of the site and the construction of an alternative dwelling in a nearby village. The Society defended its action by saying that the removal of the building would lead to a "win, win, win" situation, with the landscape being enhanced, the prospect of not one but two new dwellings being provided, and the possibility that the new houses would lead to the provision of further affordable housing in the area.

The "Revolting Peasants" were having none of it. Led by the redoubtable Molly Groves, they argued that Blackpitts Bungalow was a perfectly serviceable house in an area which badly needed homes for local people.

The protestors refused to give in even after the full National Park Authority had voted (by the narrowest possible margin, eleven votes to ten), to flatten the bungalow and clear the site. Mrs Groves and her supporters duly launched a petition and vowed to continue the battle.

The issue was eventually re-opened by the Authority and this time members voted to retain the bungalow and site, refurbish the existing dwelling up to a cost of £100,000 and let it to a local person engaged in agriculture. Following the about-turn, the Society accepted the decision, saying simply: "The Society hopes that the controversy is now diffused, since it has taken attention away from many of the other big issues facing Exmoor."

Encouraging New Generations

The role of education in fostering a better understanding and a greater appreciation among successive generations of young people growing up on Exmoor or visiting the National Park from far or near has always been given a high priority by the Society. From its earliest days the *Exmoor Review* encouraged young people from many different backgrounds to share their feelings about the moor through day and residential visits, essay and poetry competitions, and awards.

Edward Blacksell, a member of the Society from its early days, a visionary educationalist, and a great lover of Exmoor, took matters a step further in the 1960s and bought a cottage in the National Park for boys from his school to help renovate and then use for residential visits.

Blacksell was headmaster of Barnstaple County Secondary School for Boys and, unlike many of those in charge of a part of the education system catering for young people who were widely dismissed as "eleven-plus failures", he encouraged educational and recreational initiatives of many kinds. His personal association with his school was so close that the establishment was widely known as "Blacksell's Academy".

Determined to pass on his own passion for Exmoor to his charges, he bought the dilapidated Duke's Cottage at Woolhanger, near Lynton, and from the spring of 1962 onwards masters and boys worked to convert the nineteenth-century stone-walled building into a centre for outdoor activities. Standing in thirty-one acres of land in a deep, wooded valley, the amenities were primitive, with paraffin lamps, Calor gas cooking facilities and bunks for sleeping.

Blacksell, writing in the 1967 *Exmoor Review*, described the impact of the cottage and the surrounding landscape on his pupils, who were often drawn from the less prosperous areas of Barnstaple and North Devon, saying: "Undoubtedly it is the silence and the sounds that impress the boys and girls using our Exmoor cottage for their first time. Because there are no cars, no TV, and transistors [radios] are banned, at first they feel they are in a silent world. In the darkness of the first night they become aware of new sounds, creaking boards, moving trees, the rush of the stream, the cough of sheep, but, most of all, the sound of their own voices."

The Society's close connection with young people has continued and expanded. At the beginning of the twenty-first century it stepped up a gear, notably through support of the Exmoor Curriculum, introduced by Dulverton Middle School to give an opportunity for its pupils to learn about their environment and, like their predecessors from Barnstaple nearly forty years earlier, experience outdoor activities including hill walking.

Over a period of years from 2003 the Society donated more than £20,000 to Dulverton Middle School to support the curriculum. Chris Whinney, then Vice-Chairman of the Society, explained: "We identified education as a key priority for involvement and funding. We believe the Exmoor Curriculum will produce a deeper understanding of why Exmoor is a National Park and that the pupils, when they become adults, will continue to support its status."

The Society supported many other initiatives, including one very successful project that tied in with its commitment to the cultural life of Exmoor.

Barnstaple Head Teacher Edward Blacksell, a member of the Exmoor Society, bought a cottage in the National Park, near Woolhanger, for staff and pupils to renovate and then use as a base for adventure holidays. It was named Duke's Cottage because of its use for activities connected to the Duke of Edinburgh's Award scheme. (Author's Collection)

Children from Dunster School at Pinkery Outdoor Education Centre.
(Dunster School)

Chris Whinney in 2011 handing over, on behalf of the Exmoor Society, a cheque for £2,000 to Jerry Weedon, the Head Teacher of Dulverton Middle School.
(Exmoor Society)

In 2009 the Society worked with the National Park Authority to reach out to children in the area through the medium of a play designed to create a challenging vision of their inheritance. The resulting production, *Tracks and Traces – A Story of Exmoor*, used live theatre, poetry, film and state-of-the-art computerised flight simulation technology to, in the words of the producers, "switch young people on to the issues facing their environment". It was produced by The Common Players, a group with a reputation for touring environmental plays, and Means of Production Community Arts. Over a five-week period, thirty-four schools across Exmoor were visited and the production was viewed by 3,500 children. In addition, a teachers' conference involving fifty-two primary school staff was held and there were well-attended performances for the public and at the Society's annual meeting. A DVD of the play was produced and there was considerable television, radio and press coverage. The project was funded through the Exmoor National Park Authority Sustainable Development Fund and Big Lottery Awards for All.

Chris Whinney summed up the project when he told the media: "We were happy in achieving all our targets with the play, which we feel reinforced the joint kinship between ourselves and ENPA. The production also served to demonstrate the complexities that face National Parks and their people in the rapidly changing world of today."

Competitions and Awards

The early essay competitions organised by the Society were later joined by other initiatives designed to encourage the cultural life of Exmoor. Today, four competitions, run by the Society with the intention of instilling a deep feeling for Exmoor within the minds of the competitors and the public in general, are held annually, in the fields of essays, photography, children's literature and poetry.

Malcolm MacEwen, in addition to being a conservationist of international repute, wrote fluently and powerfully in support of the preservation of Exmoor and the many other causes close to his heart, and it is fitting that the Society's prestigious essay competition is named for him.

High-class photography has always been a hallmark of the *Exmoor Review* and its pages sometimes featured the work of veteran photographer Alfred Vowles. The biennial competition that bears his name is open to amateur photographers, who are invited to submit work taken on Exmoor in the two years prior to the current contest's entry date, in four categories – wildlife, landscape, heritage buildings and Exmoor activities. Each category offers a cash prize, with the overall winner receiving the Alfred Vowles Memorial Trophy, donated by his family.

Sir Antony Acland and Mary Chugg pictured on either side of Rob Wilson-North, Conservation Manager of the ENPA, when he was awarded the Mary and Brian Chugg Conservation Award in 2016.
(Exmoor Society)

Vowles was born in 1882 and, until the late 1940s, devoted his life to recording the landscape, life and people of Exmoor. For many years he ran a thriving business selling postcards of his work from a shop in Minehead, having earlier worked for Kodak in London. His legacy is a most valuable record of Exmoor of that period.

The Society's policy of encouraging young people to follow in the footsteps of the many writers and artists who over the years have been inspired by Exmoor's special qualities has produced the Lucy Perry Literary Competition, which is open to young people aged between eight and fourteen years. The competition calls for a piece of poetry or prose inspired by Exmoor. There are categories for different age groups. Whilst the contest can be used to form part of the school curriculum, entries from individuals are also welcome. The winning entries are published on the Society website and usually, when space allows, in the *Exmoor Review*.

In 2018 the Society decided to reintroduce an adult poetry competition as part of its sixtieth anniversary celebrations. As a result of the interest aroused, and more than fifty entries, it was decided to hold the competition annually. Open to anyone over the age of sixteen, poems submitted should be inspired by any aspect of Exmoor – topical, historical, archaeological, literary, recreational, spiritual or relating to flora or fauna, dark skies, or landscape.

The Society also presents three awards. The Founders' Award, sponsored by Halsgrove Publishing, was instituted in 1976, and is awarded in recognition of notable service to the Society. The 2019 award went to Hugh Thomas, for long association with the Exmoor Society. The Mary and Brian Chugg Conservation Award, formerly known as the Samuel Foss Conservation Award, is presented to people who have contributed significantly to the conservation of Exmoor. The 2019 award was presented to Adam Lockyer for his work with FWAG and Headwaters of the Exe project.

Throughout its history the Society has concerned itself with the question of employment (or lack of it) within the National Park. Despite the efforts of the Knights to industrialise Exmoor through mining and other activities, the isolation of the moor, its lack of transport facilities and its challenging terrain brought an end to their ambitions in that direction. The Pinnacle Award, set up in 2011, and explored in more detail in Chapter Nine, set out to encourage young entrepreneurs to develop businesses which would hopefully allow them to continue to live and work on Exmoor, thus escaping the fate of so many young people who have had to move elsewhere to earn a living.

SAVING THE SPLENDOUR: *The History of the Exmoor Society*

At the Big Picnic, Prince Charles was introduced to Nick Hosegood, winner of the 2017 Pinnacle Award, by Jackie Smith. (ENPA)

Prince Charles talking to trustees Anne May, Christina Williams and John Wibberley. (ENPA)

Chapter Nine
The Society Today and Tomorrow

"The founders of the Exmoor Society would have been gratified by the atmosphere of co-operation and unity apparent when the Society, the National Park Authority and the farming community, in the form of the Exmoor Hill Farming Network, combined to welcome HRH the Prince of Wales and the Duchess of Cornwall to Simonsbath. The fact that one of those founders, Mary Chugg, was present on the day was a particular delight."

Rachel Thomas, CBE, Chairman of the Exmoor Society, in 2019

The first two decades of the twenty-first century provided an ample opportunity to celebrate not only the golden and diamond anniversaries of the Exmoor Society but also a landmark occasion in the history of Britain's National Parks family. In July 2019 Exmoor was honoured to be chosen as the venue for the seventieth anniversary celebration of the passing of the 1949 Act of Parliament that led to the establishment of the National Park movement in Great Britain.

The Big Picnic

Representatives from the fifteen National Parks in England, Wales and Scotland travelled to the meadows by the River Barle at Simonsbath to join their Royal Highnesses the Prince of Wales and the Duchess of Cornwall, together with some 500 local people at that most rural form of celebration, a riverside picnic amid the glorious scenery of Exmoor.

The event was hosted by the National Park Authority in partnership with the Exmoor Society and, a newer partner, the Exmoor Hill Farming Network. In the mid-twentieth century such a coming together on a day of joyous celebration would have been unlikely to say the least, as the National Park administrators and the landowners and upland farmers who were suspicious of the motives of the Society, struggled to speak with any semblance of common purpose.

Visiting VIPs and local residents alike gave a warm welcome to the Prince of Wales and the Duchess of Cornwall on a day when the Duchess had a similar anniversary of her own to celebrate – her seventieth birthday. She marked her own special day by ceremonially cutting a celebration cake depicting various aspects of the UK's National Parks. The guests at the event heard the Prince acclaim the Parks as "places of exceptional landscapes and precious natural habitats, which provide opportunities for us all to find

Prince Charles and the Duchess of Cornwall cutting the cake representing all the National Parks. (ENPA)

peace in beauty, enhance our health and well being and explore our links with nature".

Harmony reigned, and even a late shower failed to dampen a memorable day in the history of Exmoor in particular and the National Parks movement in general. Mingling together were representatives of both Somerset and Devon County Councils and other local authorities, nearly all of whom had been vehemently opposed in the 1950s to the creation of the Exmoor Park.

There too on the day were the Lord-Lieutenant of Somerset, Mrs Anne Maw and the Lord-Lieutenant of Devon Mr David Fursdon; the High Sheriff of Somerset, Mr Johnnie Halliday; Mrs Hazel Prior-Sankey, Chairman of Somerset West and Taunton District Council; farmer Mr Robin Milton, Chairman of the Exmoor National Park Authority; Mrs Andrea Davis, Deputy Chairman of the ENPA and Devon County Council cabinet member for infrastructure, development and waste; and Mrs Frances Nicholson, Somerset County Council cabinet member for children and families, and editor of the Exmoor Society journal *Exmoor Review*.

The once hostile County Councils contributed significant funding to the event – £5,000 from Somerset and £2,500 from Devon – representing the proportional split of Exmoor's territory between Devon and Somerset, whilst the picnic had an industrial sponsor, Tarmac, represented by Mr Stuart Wykes.

Mingling convivially with the VIPs, local councillors and the people of Exmoor at the event were landowners who, for significant periods in the earlier history of the Park, would have been at daggers drawn with the Society over the issues of land use and the ploughing and afforestation of tracts of Exmoor. Rachel Thomas, Chairman of the Exmoor Society, later commented:

> As an independent charity, our aim is to protect and promote Exmoor's National Park status. The Big Picnic at Simonsbath celebrated all that makes Exmoor unique – not only its beauty, wildlife and heritage – but also upland farming livelihoods, produce from the land and the connection with nature so necessary to people's wellbeing.
>
> We were more than delighted that Their Royal Highnesses attended, recognising the national and indeed international importance of the UK's national parks for all. The event showed a local community still linked to the land with livestock, local produce and crafts, schoolchildren studying the river, country sport displays and cultural activities such as pop-up poetry, music and a resident artist all entertaining picnickers, some in splendid dress with fine hampers and rugs.
>
> Mary Chugg, the surviving member of the small group of people who founded the Exmoor Society more than sixty years ago, was present at Simonsbath on the day. I know her fellow pioneers would also have felt a sense of satisfaction through experiencing the sense of co-operation evident between the various parties with an interest in Exmoor. They would have particularly appreciated the concern apparent today amongst the Park Authority, landowners and within the Hill Farming Network, for the importance of conservation and the vital need to preserve the best of the moorland landscape.

Step Changes

For the Society, the atmosphere of cordiality and partnership working between various Exmoor stakeholders is welcome. But Society trustees, officers and members remain aware that many of the issues closest to the organisation's heart, in the areas of conservation and enjoyment of the landscape, nature and heritage, are still very much alive. The Society's roles as champion, vigilant watchdog and a critical friend of the National Park Authority and other relevant bodies must and will continue to be an absolute priority.

The two opening decades of the twenty-first century heralded a period of intense activity for the Society, which continues as the third decade approaches. Appropriately, landscape character, the fortunes of hill farming, and the issues of the effect of climate change and future land use, remain at the core of its policies and initiatives, but concern for the social and cultural life of Exmoor is also well to the forefront.

Exmoor celebrated its fiftieth year as a National Park in 2004 and the landmark anniversary was duly celebrated and, from the Society's point of view, credit given where it was deserved. But for all the achievements of past decades, there was a belief that much still needed to be done in the field of conservation, and a feeling that in the area of government priorities the importance of Exmoor and the National Park movement as a whole had been downgraded.

There was a view that the National Park authorities, at Dulverton and nationwide, had simply become part of a local government network with a regional agenda which put a particular emphasis on socio-economic regeneration, with the Parks mainly acting as test beds for the sustainable development of the countryside. The Society posed the question, 'Has Exmoor lost its way?', and the *Review* issued a rallying call, urging the Society in its role as an independent watchdog to channel its energies and enthusiasms into helping to create a vision for the National Park that looked at the bigger picture and integrated all the key interests and aspirations of the movement.

The Society commissioned and published a powerful independent report, *Moorlands at the Crossroads*, which showed that there was little consensus over the direction the moorland should take, and a worrying gap in the evidence about essential conservation interests. The *Review's* leading article in the 2006 edition issued two significant challenges designed to inspire people to see the benefits of focusing on what was special and unique about Exmoor.

The first challenge was to secure a place for Exmoor in UNESCO's list of World Heritage Sites, which included a category for cultural landscapes, defined as places where people's interaction with the natural world was measured using cultural criteria. Although the UK government had to date submitted only the Lake District and New Forest for listing, the Society believed Exmoor's ancient farmed landscape, where practices and processes for managing the moorlands had evolved slowly over time but were still relevant today, allied to the role the area had played in the early conservation movement, made it an ideal candidate. The moor's varied history and its association with art, literature, myths and legends satisfied UNESCO's cultural criteria.

At the same time the Society argued for an eventual extension of the National Park boundaries, on the basis that they had been too closely drawn to the moorland line, excluding relevant and deserving towns and villages. However, it was felt that such a move should be delayed until a simpler process for change was in place.

The desire for World Heritage Site listing has yet to be fulfilled; the second challenge issued in 2006 was always seen as longer-term, and would concentrate on firmly establishing Exmoor's special qualities. These would need to be determined in the context of National Park purposes. To progress this second challenge the Society formed a landscape advisory group to convince the National Park Authority to make available more resources to assess the condition of Exmoor's landscape.

Overall, the Exmoor Society believes that the definition of landscape requires a holistic approach. Where scenic beauty is an element, landscape means more than this as it has "layers of meaning" described as: people and nature, where sometimes the natural world appears more dominant and in other places, the influence of people is more evident; people and their history, which links past activities; people and their tangible and intangible views, which includes not only their responses to scenery and nature, but also emotional responses and associations. In other words, landscape is a social construct and expresses the inter-relationship between people and the natural world over time that gives an area a sense of place and a distinct character.

In 2007 a detailed landscape character assessment for Exmoor was undertaken and this was then updated in 2018. This now helps form key policies and provides supplementary planning guidance.

Exmoor Society Chairman Rachel Thomas explains:

> Interestingly, Devon's two National Parks are not necessarily more beautiful or capable of absorbing large numbers for outdoor recreational activities than other areas of the county. What they do have is unique combinations of special qualities, connected with their natural beauty, wildlife and cultural heritage that constitute a precious natural resource of international and global significance. As a whole they are relatively wild and tranquil, have extensive areas of open spaces and semi-natural vegetation, retain traditional systems of hill farming; in addition many of their historic landscapes are intact, with some dating from the prehistoric and medieval periods.

Employment for the Young

The encouragement of new businesses and employment opportunities for young people, to prevent where possible a drift away from the land, led to the creation of the Society's Pinnacle Award, mentioned briefly in Chapter Eight. At the award's inception Society Chairman Rachel Thomas explained: "As a conservation body, we fully recognise the importance of providing opportunities for young people to remain on the moor when they enter the world of work. We want to show that beautiful landscapes and livelihoods can go together to keep the very essence of Exmoor alive."

In view of the past importance of forges and wagon builders and repairers to Exmoor, it is notable that in 2018, when the entrants for the award were of such quality that three were chosen, each winning £3,000, one of the successful candidates was Philip Stephens, who was making a name for himself across the moor as a welder. Having started working with used horseshoes to make decorative, handcrafted garden furniture, he has now identified scope for manufacturing truck canopies and other bespoke accessories for farm and truck vehicles. In particular, he is moving towards working with lightweight aluminium rather than heavier metals.

Also very much in the metalworking tradition was the 2016 winner of the Pinnacle Award, Tom Lile, who established a business specialising in traditional ironwork, with ambitions to expand into steel fabrication to meet the needs of the modern market.

The 2015 Pinnacle Award winner, Jack Croft of Twitchen, is a prime example of how the award allows young people from Exmoor to continue to work on the land. Winning the prize allowed Jack to fulfil his dream of being able to live and work on home territory – one of the prime purposes of the prestigious scheme. Jack began to work on the land in his free time at the age of just thirteen, becoming proficient in rural skills including hedging and fencing. When he left school he immediately bought a trailer and a beaten-up old Ford tractor and worked hard to restore the vehicles to working order.

He set up a small contracting business, but his limited equipment made finding enough work to make the business viable all year round difficult. He was forced to leave Exmoor during the summer months. But this changed when he won the award.

Adding the Pinnacle cash prize to his savings from his summer jobs, he invested in new equipment, including a hydraulic post-banger attachment for his tractor, a set of chain harrows, a fertiliser spreader and a mower/conditioner. It meant he could expand his activities to also include chain sawing and mowing, all on a much bigger scale than before. But, as he explained:

Chapter Nine: The Society Today and Tomorrow

Jack Croft winner of the 2015 Pinnacle Award, pictured working on Exmoor at the hamlet of Charles. (Philip Dalling)

"The best part of it all was the knowledge that I should now be able to find enough work to stay in the area, rather than be forced to move away to find jobs. I gained a lot of experience working away and by putting in really long hours on the long summer days I could earn a decent whack of money to put towards equipment. But nothing beats living and working on Exmoor!"

Today the future is as bright as ever for Jack Croft Contracting, which now supports four people. New skills are continually being added to the business, including ground works and excavations, steep ground clearance, the erection of steel-frame buildings, baling and wrapping, spraying and re-seeding. As Jack says: "The Pinnacle Award certainly set me on the road to the sort of working life on Exmoor that had always been my ambition."

Archive and Resource Centre

The Society took another major step forward in 2014 when it moved from the Parish Rooms, Dulverton, into new premises in the heart of the town, a move made possible by the fact that the larger premises were bought by the Cave Foundation for the sole use of the Exmoor Society, enabling it to expand its activities by setting up a Resource Centre.

The writer and artist Hope Bourne was the trigger point for the realisation that the Society needed an archive resource. For more than fifty years the Society had collected a range of papers, maps, photographs, slides and reports, scattered through the two offices of its Parish Rooms headquarters. When Hope died in 2010 she left all her material, including writings, unpublished manuscripts, drawings, artefacts, books and mounds of newspaper cuttings to the Society.

The Society's trustees realised that there was a need to put all the organisation's material into some order. An archive project was launched in 2012 to raise money and employ a professional archivist starting in 2014. The facilities of the new headquarters allowed the archivist to catalogue, clean and store in environmentally controlled conditions all the material. A second project in 2016, which ended two years later, allowed the further development of the archives, to be used to protect Exmoor's special qualities. This project also made possible a new series of *Exmoor Studies*. The archive collection will continue to be publicly available with help from Society trustees and volunteers.

The Resource Centre now incorporates an extensive reference library, archive store, work-stations and free wi-fi for public use, and a display area for current material and projects such as lichen, mosses and ferns, to encourage citizen science.

Protected Landscapes

Exmoor's status as a National Park remained a major pre-occupation for the Society during the second decade of the new century and up to the present day. The organisation's continued vigilance and campaigning, backed as always by a willingness to seek expert advice from any relevant quarter, received its reward with the publication of the most recent major study into the National Parks sector.

The 2019 Society annual meeting coincided with the long-awaited publication of the report on the future of National Parks, titled *Landscapes Review*. The *Review*, led by the author Julian Glover, was described by the commissioning body, the Department for Environment, Agriculture and Food as "potentially the biggest shake-up in the running of the country's

Chapter Nine: The Society Today and Tomorrow

Part of the Exmoor Society Archive and Resource Centre. (Philip Dalling)

National Parks and Areas of Outstanding Natural Beauty since they were founded more than seventy years ago".

Glover and his panel toured all forty-four Parks and AONBs during the preparation of the *Review*, with Exmoor among the first to receive a visit, in July 2019. On the evening before meeting various interest groups with the Exmoor Park, Glover hosted a dinner at Tarr Farm Inn, where the guests included Exmoor Society Chairman Rachel Thomas. The eventual publication called for bold action to reignite the founding spirit of the National Park movement, to make the Parks greener, more beautiful and open to everyone.

When *Landscapes Review* was published, the Exmoor Society was delighted to find that many of the points it had made to the panel had been fully developed in the final document. Examples included the report's call for a National Landscape Service to be set up to promote National Parks and AONBs as a family at the national level; changes in governance at a National Park level, with smaller boards; more space for nature and greater access for all; and a new agri-environmental scheme with greater local flexibility, in the case of Exmoor designed to enable farmers to remain on the moor and continue their traditional practices.

Julian Glover, author of the report on the future of National Parks, toured Exmoor whilst preparing the review. He is pictured (left) *at Lynmouth about to ride the Cliff Railway to Lynton.* (ENPA)

At the Spring Conference in 2017 Professor Dieter Helm, Chairman of the Natural Capital Committee, challenged the Society to explore how best the concept could be employed in practice, by compiling a register of Exmoor's natural capital assets. Professor Helm is pictured (centre) *with Society Chairman Rachel Thomas and President Sir Antony Acland.* (Exmoor Society)

Landscapes Review also fully recognised the Exmoor Society's important work in relation to the new concept of natural capital. Professor Dieter Helm, Chairman of the Natural Capital Committee, challenged the Society to explore how best the concept could be employed in practice, by compiling a register of Exmoor's natural capital assets. The *Review* acknowledged that the Society had immediately risen to this challenge, starting with a project to trial a practical "tool-kit" that would help identify eco-system services provided by Exmoor. This was tested in three pilot areas which between them covered all the landscape types in the Exmoor National Park. Glover acknowledged that this initiative by the Society had significantly moved forward the natural capital concept.

The Society's view was that the trial had advanced the natural capital approach in several ways: by proposing a unifying classification of all elements of natural capital; by investigating and describing the relationship between natural capital and cultural considerations (previously frequently neglected); by using landscape character to ensure descriptions of natural capital are place-based, capturing the distinctiveness and special qualities of landform, land cover, management and perceptions; and, finally, by demonstrating the importance of involving local knowledge and values to gain the commitment of the people who own, manage or use natural capital, giving them a personal stake in the concept.

The Exmoor Society in turn praised the work undertaken on its behalf by the consultancy Rural Focus, and welcomed its report, *Towards a Register of Exmoor's Natural Capital*. It also welcomed *A Green Future: Our 25 Year Plan to Improve the Environment*, the UK government's long-term approach to protecting and enhancing the UK's natural landscape, habitats and heritage, which set natural capital at its heart. The Rural Focus findings accepted that, on Exmoor, farmers played a key role in creating, enhancing and maintaining the visual landscape so greatly enjoyed and valued by visitors and residents alike. In part, this landscape stems from extensive sheep and cattle livestock farming which uses the moorland, and partly from farmers in a role as stewards of the wider countryside. They also provide holiday and recreational facilities and, with their families, are the bedrock of a great deal of Exmoor's social life and traditions.

A Rallying Cry for the Future

On the brink of the third decade of the twenty-first century, and with environmental concerns coming ever closer to the forefront of national and global affairs, veteran conservationist Dame Fiona Reynolds, now Master of Emmanuel College, Cambridge, paid a welcome return to Dunster for the 2019 Spring Conference, 'Inspirational Exmoor'. She had a message for those present and for the wider national audience with an interest in,

Spring Conference: Major Issues and Expert Speakers

A wide range of issues of importance to Exmoor have for many years been identified, analysed and debated annually at the Society's Spring Conferences. At first, attendance was limited to members. By 2006, when the reputation of the event had grown in importance, the general public was welcomed. Topics covered the gamut of Exmoor issues with a wide range of speakers with academic and practical expertise in many fields including environmentalists, conservationists, and tourism providers – one of the reasons why the knowledgeable Exmoor commentator Martin Hesp, formerly of the *Western Morning News* was able to state categorically that the Society "punched above its weight".

An early topic was 'The Future of Farming on Exmoor' which brought together a variety of people, including Helen Phillips, the Chief Executive Officer of Natural England, Exmoor Farmer Guy Thomas-Everard, Dr Janet Dyer, Reader in Rural Studies at the Universities of Gloucester and the West of England, John Waldon of the South West Uplands Federation, and Allan Buckwell, Professor of Agricultural Economics and the County Landowners Association Director of Policy.

Over the years other topics for the conferences have included energy planning, Exmoor's Heritage – in terms of archaeology, historic buildings, and the cultural riches of the National Park, Exmoor's rivers and woodlands – and the future of the landscape. Speakers have included Dieter Helm, Professor of Energy Policy at Oxford University, on Exmoor's natural capital; Malcolm Bell, Chief Executive of South West Tourism Ltd, on the economic importance of visitors; the ENPA Chief Executive Nigel Stone on the management of tourism; Lee Bray, Historic Environment Officer for the Exmoor Mires Project, on archaeological discoveries on Exmoor; Mike Bishop of Active Exmoor on activity holidays, and the Exmoor environmentalist Stanley Johnson reflected the view of an Exmoor resident.

The 2019 Spring Conference, 'Inspirational Exmoor', addressed the issues of Natural Beauty and People's Wellbeing. The speakers included Dame Fiona Reynolds, former Director of the National Trust (see pages 119 and 121), and Peter Beacham, a former Devon County Council Historic Buildings Advisor and later Director of Heritage Protection at English Heritage. Lending a more specifically West Country accent were Rob Wilson-North, Head of Conservation and Access at the ENPA, Adrian Colston, a PhD researcher at the Centre for Rural Policy Research at the University of Exeter, and Matt Heard, Natural England's Area Manager for Somerset. The talks were interspersed with Adam Horovitz reading poems he had written during visits to Exmoor farms and included in his book *The Soil Never Sleeps*.

and a deep commitment to, the concept of the conservation of areas of outstanding natural beauty.

Dame Fiona regretted the fact that lobbyists, politicians – and those responsible for making the decisions in the area of rural policy – leant too heavily on technical terms rather than words such as beauty, nature and heritage. People, she insisted, understood what was beautiful – "a stunning view, a heath fritillary butterfly, an ancient stone circle" and closeness to nature with good access to outstanding natural landscapes was crucial to society's wellbeing. It was, she added, essential to redress the dramatic loss of biodiversity and recognise the vulnerability of landscape beauty. "The fight for beauty must continue," she said, "even in National Parks."

Undoubtedly, the Exmoor Society will continue to champion the National Park concept. It will also continue to fulfil its role as an effective watchdog and on occasions say things that others will not. As a voluntary body and independent charity, very much a membership body, with just 1.4 equivalent employees, the Society will remain highly dependent upon the calibre of its trustees, officers and volunteers.

As an evidence-based organisation seeking solutions to a variety of problems, some of which will, at any one time, not be considered fashionable, the Society will continue to be intimately concerned with the integration of the environment and socio-economic issues, particularly where there is an effect upon livelihoods on Exmoor.

In response to Dame Fiona's plea, the Society can validly claim constantly to engage with current and imminent policy issues that may impinge on the vital qualities of Exmoor and the wellbeing of its various communities – the farmers who live and work there, others who depend directly and indirectly for a livelihood earned in the National Park, retired people in search of tranquility, those wanting a place to enjoy sport and recreation and, not least, residents and visitors who value the protection and conservation of Exmoor's unique and beautiful semi-natural environment for the benefit of future generations. Above all, the Society aims to communicate with all constituencies clearly and effectively, as far as possible translating technical terms into language everyone can understand. Reference to the *Exmoor Review* is evidence of that approach. Only then can the Society fulfil its purpose of influencing decisions based on informed opinion, widely shared, and so most likely to lead to good outcomes.

For sure, the Society will be needed even more in the future and is prepared to face the challenges that undoubtedly lie ahead. It will continue to closely monitor each and every new national and international initiative with any relevance to the National Park. National Parks in general will be buffeted by these changes with great pressure being exerted from single-issue groups, polarised debate and inbuilt conflict in purposes. The Society will need to become increasingly involved with climate change and resilience issues, prioritising nature recovery but not neglecting other crucial elements of National Park purposes. Land use will continue to be a major issue, particularly in the context of increasing demand for recreational facilities. Associated with this will be acceptance of the fact that Exmoor has capacity for additional woodland areas, provided these are well-planned, well-situated and environmentally acceptable. A further issue of major importance will centre around increasing the diversity of the people drawn to Exmoor and the other UK National Parks; the Exmoor Society firmly believes that diversity is a more important factor than sheer numbers alone.

Without question, the Exmoor Society is ready to tackle the future on all fronts, energised by its rich heritage and present activities, where it believes it can make a difference to Exmoor as a National Park and, as the title aptly chosen for this history asserts, helping to save the splendour.

Exmoor Society Spring Conference at Dulverton in 2019. Left to right: Adrian Colston, Matthew Heard, Rob Wilson-North, Rachel Thomas, Robin Milton, Dame Fiona Reynolds, Sir Antony Acland, Sarah Bryan, Adam Horovitz, Jill Edwards, Peter Beacham. (Philip Dalling)

Select Bibliography

Victor Bonham-Carter, *The Essence of Exmoor*, The Exmoor Press, 1991.

────── *What Countryman, Sir?*, B-C Press, 1996.

Hope L. Bourne, *Living on Exmoor*, Galley Press, 1963. Revised edition published by Exmoor Books 1991.

S.H. Burton, *Exmoor*, Westaway, 1952.

────── *Exmoor*, Hodder & Stoughton, 1969 (some material taken from 1952 book); Robert Hale, 2nd ed. 1974, 3rd ed. 1978, 4th ed.1984.

Hazel Eardley-Wilmot, *Yesterday's Exmoor*, Exmoor Books, 1990.

L.V. Grinsell, *The Archaeology of Exmoor*, David & Charles, 1970.

E.R. Lloyd, *The Wild Red Deer of Exmoor*, Exmoor Press, 1970; 2nd ed. 1975.

Ann & Malcolm MacEwen, *National Parks: Conservation or Cosmetics?*, George Allen & Unwin, 1982.

────── *Greenprints for the Countryside? The story of Britain's National Parks*, Allen & Unwin, 1982.

Malcolm MacEwen, *The Greening of a Red*, Pluto Press, 1991.

C.S. Orwin, R. Sellick and V. Bonham-Carter, *The Reclamation of Exmoor Forest*, Oxford University Press 1929; 2nd ed. David & Charles, 1970; 3rd ed. and with further revisions and additional chapter by V. Bonham-Carter, Exmoor Books,1997.

J.H.B. Peel, *Portrait of Exmoor*, Robert Hale, 1970.

F.H. Snell, *A Book of Exmoor*, Methuen, 1903. Facsimile Edition published by Halsgrove, 2002.

In the preparation of this book extensive use has been made of the Exmoor Society Archives, press releases and newspaper cuttings, library holdings and major reports published by the Society individually or in partnership with other organisations.

SAVING THE SPLENDOUR: The History of the Exmoor Society

SAVING THE SPLENDOUR: *The History of the Exmoor Society*

View from Webber's Post to Cloutsham and the west. (Leanna Coles)

Philip Dalling. (Devon Life)

Note on the Author

Philip Dalling was born and has spent much of his life in Derbyshire, where the accessibility of the Peak District first awakened his interest in National Parks. His family can trace its links to the village of Swimbridge in North Devon back to the late-seventeenth century and a love of Exmoor was fostered by many holiday visits to the moor and the Bristol Channel coastline. He has worked as a newspaper journalist and in press relations in industry and the Government Information Service. He was for twenty-two years Director of Public Affairs at The University of Nottingham. On making his home in North Devon he returned to his journalistic roots, working as a freelance contributor to the *North Devon Journal* and other newspapers and magazines. For seven years he wrote the 'Man on the Moor' column for *Devon Life*, covering Exmoor topics, and he continues to contribute to the magazine.